IN A NEW LIGHT

Spirituality and the Media Arts

Ron Austin

WILLIAM B. EERDMANS PUBLISHING COMPANY

GRAND RAPIDS, MICHIGAN / CAMBRIDGE, U.K.

Published 2007 by
Wm. B. Eerdmans Publishing Co.
2140 Oak Industrial Drive N.E., Grand Rapids, Michigan 49505 /
P.O. Box 163, Cambridge CB3 9PU U.K.

Printed in the United States of America

12 11 10 09 08 07   7 6 5 4 3 2 1

Library of Congress Cataloging-in-Publication Data

Austin, Ron.
    In a new light: spirituality and the media arts / Ron Austin.
        p.   cm.
    Includes index.
    ISBN 978-0-8028-0773-1 (pbk.: alk. paper)
    1. Mass media in religion.   2. Motion pictures — Religious aspects.
    I. Title.

    BL638.A97   2007
    201′.67914 — dc22

                                      2007027548

www.eerdmans.com

Contents

Introduction

Writing this book has been an act of faith. After nearly a half century in Hollywood, first as a young actor, then as a writer and producer, and finally as a teacher, this faith has been shaped and tested in the "real world" of the media industry. I am not a theorist; I'm a survivor.

Decades of life in Hollywood have left me all too familiar with the fear and anxieties at its core — the fear of failure, of course, but also the deeper fears of falling short of one's hopes and expectations, and, ultimately, of neglect and disregard.

As my younger colleagues report, Hollywood is still a fear-ridden town. The old ties of liberal belief and artistic aspiration have frayed, and while long-nurtured friendships survive, the fellowship that I knew at studio commissary tables and Sunset Strip bars in the fifties and sixties is largely gone. Much of this is due to changes mandated by technology and economics. Hollywood was once a provincial company town in which the privileged workers referred simply to "the Industry" and outsiders as "civilians," or, in the argot of *Variety*, "non-pros." Now it's a banana republic ruled by interests largely foreign to its inhabitants and their dreams, and run by managers who view the "talent" as products on an assembly line — and as replaceable. Careers, even at the top, have grown as short as those of baseball relief pitchers.

This loss of continuity and community, always fragile, has only increased the anxiety about the future. It was always a tough town, as ruthlessly competitive as a gold rush, but once inside the gates, there were ties that lasted and, however grudging, a respect for talent. It is still a tough town, but, increasingly, a cold and lonely one.

"Hollywood" isn't just a place; it's a state of mind. Young filmmakers around the world face the challenge of living and working in this competitive environment. This challenge is at the heart of what I want to write about. Not in regret or condemnation. I don't want to bring back the "old Hollywood" for all its glamour. What's needed isn't nostalgia, but a new spirit. I want young filmmakers, wherever they are, to become truly independent and, once again, inspired and hopeful.

A new generation of media artists — writers, directors, actors, musicians, and technicians — must determine how to use the new freedom made possible by technology. This is the new frontier; but to cross it we must find the courage and spiritual resources to move beyond fear. As with any pioneering generation, this will entail sacrifice. To make this effort, we must overcome fears of personal failure. We must sustain a greater vision, beyond careers, one that serves others, whose stories must be told if we are to understand the meaning of our own.

We will need a strong faith to make the sacrifices this exploration requires. The new generation of media artists must, as the cultural historian George Steiner has urged, be prepared to "gamble on transcendence." This gamble involves high risk, and that's why I call this book an act of faith.

To sustain hope against the odds, in Hollywood or anywhere else, is a spiritual challenge. Therefore much of this book explores a spiritual foundation for creative work. It is based upon my search as a teacher for some common-ground principles upon which we might build creative relationships. I'm not, however, seeking to replace traditional religious belief. I have sought an inclusive path, not an esoteric one. I've looked for what we already share and might build upon.

An authentic spirituality entails ethics — essentially, how we treat other people. One of the central questions that came out of my workshops over the years was, then, how to apply these basic principles to the personal relationships involved in filmmaking. Was it possible to make films in a way that could break out of the ego-driven limits of domination and still allow individual expression?

This eventually became the basis of an experiment, the goal of which was to liberate the individual through a collaborative process similar to jazz: an ensemble creating a structure that fosters individual freedom. An appendix tells of this experiment and continues the exploration.

As we proceed, my dependence upon inspirational figures such as Chiara Lubich, René Girard, and Martin Buber will become as evident as my own limitations. I trust that I have been faithful to their teaching; but this, too, is an act of faith.

PART ONE

Spiritual Foundations

In searching for a spiritual foundation for creative work, three principles, common to all the faith traditions, emerged:

- *Being in the Present Moment,*

- *Affirming the Mystery of the Other,* and

- *Transforming Conflict.*

The First Principle:
Being in the Present Moment

"Writing is like giving birth: we cannot help making the supreme effort. But I need have no fear of not making the supreme effort — provided only that I am honest with myself and that I pay attention."

SIMONE WEIL

B efore an audience can see a film, it must be awake. Yet people frequently view movies without really "seeing" anything. This is because they are not spiritually awake. If they are not brought awake, then the people who made the film were probably asleep as well. In fact, the movie may have been made by people who were asleep for people who don't want to wake up.

This is the problem that I believe Simone Weil, a unique blend of classics scholar and mystic, addresses when she relates being honest with "paying attention," another term for "being in the moment."

If we want to "wake up," to be fully alive and aware of the challenge before us as artists, we must try to understand the nature of our perpetual "sleep." To overcome this sleep is, fundamentally, a spiritual matter, and to come awake requires the practice of one of the most universal and ancient spiritual disciplines.

At the heart of this discipline, in all its varieties, is the daunting task of emptying ourselves of our desires and preconceptions. This opens our eyes as writers, actors, and filmmakers so that we can truly "see" the characters we create, and, as we will find, opens us to the sacred origins of life and art.

The practice of "being in the present moment" or "attention" can be animated by reciting traditional prayers, such as the "Jesus Prayer" of the Eastern Orthodox, the Rosary, the ritual daily prayers of Judaism, the ninety-nine names of Allah, or a Buddhist mantra. It is a practice at the heart of religious culture. All traditional religions have spiritual practices designed simply to awaken us to reality, to the goodness of life and, on the other hand, to the illusions of desire. For Christians, Jews, and Muslims, it is an encounter with the fullness of Being, the One called God.

I have stressed what I consider to be the irreducible spiritual character of this kind of awareness; but my experience with media artists such as writers and actors suggests that this practice is closely related to the inner discipline inherent in artistic creativity. The liberation of imagination and energy that is the fruit of this practice is not limited to, or by, religious belief.

This practice is not, in any case, simply a matter of the repetition of prayerful words. It has more to do with a kind of listening, an inner receptivity, than mere verbalization. A radical openness to the divine or sacred is a universal experience; yet it is a goal that eludes the ordinary categories of thought. As with food or color or the delights of music, this is a "real presence," powerful in its effects but not reducible to conceptual analysis.

There is a Japanese Zen expression that suggests the essence of this "present moment" experience. The term is translated literally as "become no-thought," or "the place of no-thought." Being in the present moment means going to the place of no-thought, the place of silent prayer and creative imagination. It is a path to the integrated center of our being.

And the only way to go there, so to speak, is to *be* there.

In establishing our spiritual foundations, our common ground, our first question must then be: How can we wake up? We cannot simply be taught to do this, for, paradoxically, the objective is to have no objective. One can only be pointed in a direction that is natural to the one truly seeking it. The result is a kind of detachment, a radical emptying of one's self. The goal of not having a goal is radical receptivity.

Though varying in practice, the many traditions suggest that to achieve this radical openness, we must do the following:

We must first recognize that we don't really know how to see or listen. Once we admit this disability as part of our human condition and are motivated to overcome it, we must then practice simply being present. This is not mere "self-improvement," but a daily effort that involves the body, mind, and spirit.

We must also recognize that there are many different approaches to the present moment.
Being in the present moment is a holistic exercise that incorporates all aspects of life. It may encompass meditation, prayer, work, exercise, breathing, diet, and spiritual reading. We must discern which path is most suitable for us. Conducting this search, going to the roots of a tradition can help us to know who we really are, and are meant to be. If we search together as collaborative artists, with mutual respect, this can help us find a common language and, importantly, lessen competition and rivalry.

Being in the present moment is now used, quite properly, as a part of the training of actors, and the truth of a performance is grounded in this discipline. However, the term "present moment" has, in recent years, become something of a cliché. However useful in the arts, this practice is fundamentally spiritual and, as such, is far more demanding than acquiring mere artistic technique. Whatever the specific practice, if it is authentic, it will provoke strong resistance; for being in the present moment induces the insight that all action is based upon the universal principle of self-sacrifice. Everything alive is designed to give way, to yield itself to what is to be born.

Attention as "self-emptying" inescapably involves negation. It requires loss and suffering. We must, therefore, expect inner resistance, and remain aware of it. In fact, the observation of our various forms of resistance can lead to a greater self-understanding.

I believe that the best of filmmaking is a kind of revelation made possible by an attentive "seeing in the moment"; but it also requires a willingness of the creative artist to risk and suffer along with the characters. We shall explore this further in the next chapter.

The first principle, then, leads us to observe that, far more than a lack of skill, the obstacle to good writing, directing, and acting is inattentiveness.

If you are aware that you are rarely awake, you're beginning to wake up.

The Second Principle:
Affirming the Mystery of the Other

"The 'thou' signifies all that you have been, could be, or will be."

MARTIN BUBER

The true test of our morality as filmmakers lies in the way that we treat our characters. Do we treat the characters that we create as "objects" to be manipulated for our own purposes, or do we attempt to give them life by allowing them to have a depth of being? As we direct the encounters between characters, are we ourselves open to the possibility of surprise and change? How we imagine these encounters, the way in which we see, hear, and react to one another, is the key test of what we sought in "being in the present moment": The Other reveals our capacity to see and hear.

According to Martin Buber, the Jewish sage and author of *I and Thou*, we relate to each other by either abstracting the other person into an "it" — identified by roles and functions — or we encounter the other as "thou," a fellow human being who can never be fully grasped nor controlled.

The "it" person is seen merely in terms of traits, characteristics, and patterns of behavior. The "thou" person, in Buber's terms, is one whom we accept as a mystery full of possibility.

The "I/It" relationship, while functional, is based on sameness, on predictable patterns. "I/It" as a basis of relationship may be necessary in life, but if it becomes the persistent mode, as Buber writes, it "eliminates the soul." We come to see our very identity as formed by a pattern of expectations. "I/It" can never deal with uniqueness, and our human wholeness is unique. The truth of the "Thou" is that it is always emergent and becoming.

Similarly, the truth of the characters and dialogue that we create is based upon our openness to non-manipulated, reciprocal encounters. We must be open to everything that can be "seen" in the Other, the fullness in all the characters.

This nonjudgmental openness to others, more intuitive than objective, has risks and can leave us defenseless. Just as we resist the nakedness of the "present moment," we resist this openness, preferring an often-spurious sense of control.

Many writers will testify that when the characters they create come alive, they become dangerously unpredictable! Yet here is where we must "risk transcendence"; we come awake to our own wholeness only by confronting the wholeness of others.

At the heart of the "I/Thou" encounter is the possible creation of new meaning. New meaning is not just better understanding, but a form of revelation.

In teaching screenwriting, I've found it curious how seldom we examine the nature of human dialogue and how it actually occurs. From observation I believe that a good writer knows some, if not most of this intuitively. I think the good writer knows something like the following:

Good dialogue requires "listening of a different order."
Before anything is written, there is a listening between the lines, hearing the significance of silence, or hearing how a misperception of intent, spoken or not, can lead to new meaning, sometimes created on the spot.

Genuine dialogue has no guaranteed results.
Merely functional language will kill drama — as well as relationships. The "thou-moments" in which the Other is suddenly truly "seen" are described by Martin Buber as "uncanny" and evoke mystery. This mystery is what gives richness to characterization.

Authentic dialogue is prevented by a lack of forgiveness.
Truthful characterization is doomed by a lack of forgiveness, the judg-

ments we impose on our characters; but it can also include the unconscious lack of forgiveness of one's self.

It seems to me that many contemporary writers, however talented, impose their own limitations, even despair on their characters. If truthful, this can create powerful drama. If, on the other hand, it is merely a fashionable cynicism, then it is as evasive as any shallow optimism.

The mystery of the Other is at the heart of dialogue, in life and in films. It is the mystery of ourselves as found in the Other, and yet more.

The Third Principle:
Transforming Conflict

T he moral obligation of the artist is to transform conflict in such a way that it forces us to delve into the fundamental sources of conflict and violence. This requires a sincere effort to take a conflict, in art or life, to the deepest possible level, where it can be shared and better understood.

Our objective, then, is not to resolve or avoid conflict, but to be able to truly and fully observe and probe it.

Conflict arises out of our desire to control change. We begin to understand conflict by first observing this pattern in ourselves. Human beings both desire change and resist it; but most of all, we want to control it. Our inner conflicts only intensify as our efforts to impose our will upon the world are inevitably frustrated. These inner conflicts are then projected onto others. This, one might say, is the beginning of drama.

We cannot halt change, we can rarely direct it, but we can observe it. Anthony de Mello comments: "[T]o understand what you are requires complete freedom from all desire to change what you are into something else." Thus, he concludes, "change will not be brought about by your cunning, restless ego that is forever competing, comparing, coercing, sermonizing, manipulating."

In making this effort to observe conflict as a process at work, we are not proposing an exercise in moral relativism. We must recognize our moral obligations; we have an obligation to be "right" if being right means recognizing truth and seeking justice. The question for filmmakers is how to learn to be right in a way that creates a loving detachment open to an even deeper truth.

Let's consider three fundamental sources of conflict, which we will term *ignorance and error*, the *mirroring process*, and *perversity or malevolence*.

Factual ignorance and error are prevalent but do not create in themselves lasting conflict. If a fictional conflict is based upon mere misunderstanding, it is inherently weak and ineffective. It can be the basis of farce, but not drama.

The most common form of sustained conflict is the "mirroring" of inner, unresolved disharmonies. Mirroring reveals the Other deeply imbedded, though hidden, in ourselves, or qualities in the Other which we lack. Fear and resentment are overt sources of conflict and violence. However, much of our fear and resentment come from our own fundamental internal divisions, which we project onto others.

The turning point in the process of transforming conflict into drama is invariably the revelation and acceptance of our own contradictions.

The possibility of the transformation of these mirrored conflicts — in life or films — means the willingness to recognize the Other, whether concealed or missing in ourselves.

The revelation is to discover in our adversaries the mirror of our own projections, images, and missing pieces. The very attempt to make this discovery is an act of humility. To proceed requires trust. The result is compassion.

I believe that an insight into the inner sources of conflict, our desires and fears concealed from ourselves, gives force and added significance to Jesus' admonition that we must "love our enemies."

Predictably, there is serious inner resistance to this process as there is to all of our spiritual principles.

Our conflicts are often related to our group loyalties, and their transformation can be threatening to identity itself. As with the other principles, the transformation of conflict means freeing ourselves, emptying ourselves so that we can then be open to the mystery of others, including their suffering.

Do we really welcome this? Of course not. Most often we must be dragged kicking and screaming into self-transcendence.

When we find ourselves in conflict due to perversity or malevolence, analysis becomes difficult. And when we are in conflict with someone we see as an enemy, a destroyer who threatens our very being or identity, we are then confronting the question of evil.

Transforming Conflict, Part II:
The Question of Evil

"If reality administers a hard enough shock to awaken us for an instant, by contact with a saint, for instance . . . it is then and only then that we feel for a moment the horrible monotony of evil and the unfathomable marvel of good."

SIMONE WEIL

Evil is impossible to define. It is only accessible through myth, symbol, and story. It is similar to what we've called being in the present moment, or the mystery of the Other, in that we experience it, but can't confine it conceptually.

Evil is experienced as death, suffering, guilt, alienation, sin — but is more than any one word can imply. It suggests the abyss of meaninglessness as well as the merciless law of fate.

The traditional religious view in the West is that God does not create evil, but, mysteriously, permits it. Evil pertains to a deeper reality. Evil can even reveal the Good that is the Mystery of God. Without a belief in God, evil is experienced as meaninglessness, the random effects of a more fundamental chaos, or, conversely, implies a mindless, inhuman fixity.

No matter what our creedal belief, if one does not believe that the universe is, in some way, fundamentally ordered, then evil is a meaningless concept. Yet human beings experience something so fundamental, so negating and threatening, that no other word seems to suffice. To most of us, evil remains as real as pain and death.

To grasp evil as storytellers, we must relate the question of evil to our own lives and experience. My own experience, serving in my later years as a prison chaplain in a maximum-security facility, meant daily encounters with evil as gratuitous violence and self-destructive addictions.

These behaviors were concrete, extreme, and often beyond my comprehension. I remember an extensive interview with a handsome, highly articulate young man who had sexually assaulted and murdered several children. I confess that I was unable to begin to fathom the crimes he freely admitted. I could only stand at the edge of his darkness and pray for his victims, and for him. I was encountering evil and knew it, and I remain humbled by the experience.

A woman inmate offered her own interpretation of evil in Fred Alford's book *What Evil Means to Us,* based upon interviews with prison inmates: "Evil people don't just want to hurt you, they want to hurt you from the inside." Evil, Alford concluded, comes from our effort to "cheat" our own pain, vulnerability, and death by somehow inflicting it on others.

This insight suggests that, particularly in the media age, the imagined killing of others may at least temporarily lessen the fear of death. Films can also provide symbolic forms by which we can examine evil in ways that do not inflict it on others. However, these depictions are of no value when they merely mirror our dread.

Portrayals of evil in the media can overwhelm us. Instead of interpreting evil, giving it significant form, so to speak, most films imitate and some even celebrate evil, and, in the long run, confuse and desensitize us.

But how, then, should we depict evil?

I believe that the key lies in our attitude toward suffering. The "answer" to evil lies not in avoiding suffering but accepting it, as with death, as part of the human condition and allowing it to guide us. Simone Weil contends that classical tragedies such as those of Euripides or Shakespeare can properly be called sacred art when the work "consecrates a love for the good that is found only in the depths of affliction." This means that if we are to cope with evil in any art form, we are challenged to transform it through truth and faith. In our times, I believe that this will require us to rediscover the sacred roots of art.

In seeking the sacred in art, however, we must be mindful of presumptions that can lead us to prefer or even substitute the strong emotions produced by drama for virtue or wisdom. Art can deceive us, as philosopher Iris Murdock warns, by making us "feel that we are already wise and good." Even at its highest, art is not a shortcut to virtue or wisdom. We must remember that God's "art works" are people.

We need, then, to proceed with faith and humility. If our story compels us to confront evil, we should tell the story only, so to speak, on our knees.

Transforming Conflict, Part III:
The Moral Challenge of the "Heavy"

"Once upon a time a temple and an altar on which the victim was sacrificed were substituted for the original act of collective violence; now there is an amphitheater and a stage."

RENÉ GIRARD

A temple and altar, then a stage, and now . . . the movies.
Conflict and violence are an inevitable consequence of the human condition, and it is the filmmaker's ethical obligation to tell the truth. But what is the full truth about violence? What truth does violence unveil? These are the hard questions addressed by the noted scholar René Girard, whose groundbreaking work provides a cogent interpretation of the baffling interplay of culture, violence, and religion.

Gil Bailie, author of *Violence Unveiled,* explicates the challenging theories of Girard and applies them to the present-day media. Bailie claims that the causes of the growing excesses of media violence reach back into the origins of drama itself. Ultimately, he argues, we will not fully appreciate what is at stake until the ancient ritual roots of the dramatic arts are exposed.

The origin of theater, Bailie reminds us, is in ritual sacrifice. While ultimately "mythified," these dramatizations were, in fact, reenactments of prior social crises resolved by the sacrifice of a "scapegoat" victim. Girard's central thesis is that it is the death of an actual victim that resolves violent social crises — and, therefore, makes human culture possible. Archaic culture came from these acts of violence, experienced by its participants as sacred events, which they subsequently reenacted in dramatic ritual.

Archaic societies came into being by solving this conflict born of relentless rivalry, and they did so through the scapegoating process. By remembering the violent act mythologically, our ancestors invented the stabilizing force of primitive religion.

Sacrifice is, then, the religious root of drama. What this analysis reveals is that vestiges of bloody ritual survive in the arts of theater and film today. This is most evident in the ubiquitous presence of the convenient and expendable villain that in Hollywood is called "the heavy."

René Girard's essential insight is that human desire is based on envy and imitation, what he refers to as "mimetic desire." This is the desire of two or more people for an object, person, or status, which leads to rivalry, and then, inescapably, to conflict and violence. The resolution and containment of this rivalrous violence is a prerequisite for human survival.

Girard and Bailie's most useful and provocative insight for us as filmmakers is that mimetic desire and rivalry are also at the heart of contemporary media culture.

The rituals of the ancient world and the enticements of the contemporary media are not so far apart as time might suggest.

And the key figure to our understanding of both is the "scapegoat."

The central event in the Christian story of redemption is the crucifixion of Jesus, a scapegoating event structurally identical to every scapegoating event in history. But it is depicted in a way — and this is important — that *radically contradicts mythological interpretations.* For the crucifixion exposes the truth about the sacrificial system that archaic myths and rituals conceal: *The victim is innocent and the victimizers are intoxicated by their own violence.*

By exposing this system of blood sacrifice to moral scrutiny, the crucifixion precipitated what Bailie calls "the greatest anthropological shift of imagination in history." By revealing the truth about scapegoating, the Passion of Jesus becomes the hidden foundation of contemporary drama. It rips apart the curtain that concealed the *deus ex machina* of previous dramatic catharsis.

There is now, however, a contradiction at the heart of modern, at least

Western civilization. The essence of the Christic story compels us, whatever our creed, to view the face of the innocent victim. We can no longer turn away. But the outrage we feel about victimization, the suffering of the innocent, has blinded us to our own victimizing ways.

In countless films and TV programs, we continue to pillory those whom we now regard as victimizers. The scapegoat mechanism is alive and well in Hollywood; only the "heavies" change from time to time.

The contradiction this analysis reveals is that *the good, which expels evil, can easily become an accomplice in the continuing reign of evil.*

Trying to rid the world of victimizers, we have conjured up a new community of victims, and this tendency is increased by the fact, demonstrated throughout history, that those who have been scapegoated are often the most inclined to inflict the practice on others. Awakening from the seductive power of this ceremony of false innocence is the central moral challenge of our age. Contemporary filmmakers face this crisis of conscience as much, or more than anyone else in modern culture.

The filmmaker or writer may have a wide variety of narrative options, but when it comes to resolving conflict, the options dwindle. Ultimately, there are only two. The first option is the ancient and still most popular one of purging the community of its violence by assigning its sin to a scapegoat.

The other option, far more difficult, is for us to be made aware of our own complicity in the sinfulness and delusion of the protagonists. If a drama does not lead us to the discovery that our own lives are as enmeshed as those of the protagonists in desire and delusion, then we will either have to purge our complicity at the expense of someone else, or wallow in self-loathing and the despairing assumption that there is no way out. Extricating ourselves from this moral hall of mirrors is infinitely challenging. It is the challenge that any serious filmmaker must now face.

The Search for Unity

"... [N]o experiment in art is valuable unless it is psychologically necessary. ... The innovator is 'driven on,' step by step, in his innovations, by an inner necessity. ... The novelty of form has been rather forced upon him by his material than deliberately sought. Such an inner necessity is connected with the whole history of the age in which the poet lives. ... Any radical change in poetic form is likely to be a symptom of some very much deeper change in society and in the individual."

T. S. ELIOT

The primary criterion we should consider in evaluating all art, including films, is integrity. As the word suggests, what we seek is a oneness, a unifying consistency, but also an integrity of purpose, an honesty. We admire integrity in art because we know how difficult it is to achieve.

An extended principle, *the unity of form and content,* has traditionally provided the basis of art criticism and analysis. The artist's ability to find the form that most completely expresses an insight, whose work most aptly "signifies" truth and beauty, deserves our highest esteem.

More important than providing a critical principle, recognizing the need for formal unity can steer artists away from a dualism that cripples their craft by deceiving them into thinking that the content, "the message," can somehow justify an inadequate form, or, conversely, that formal innovation is simply invention or novelty.

In judging a film, for instance, the unity principle asserts that there is no way to separate what the film "says" from how it says it. As I. A. Richards observed about poetry, what matters is not what a poem says, but *what it is.* Flannery O'Connor made the same observation about fiction: "The whole story is the meaning, because it is an experience, not an abstraction."

It is a misreading of a film as a work of art if we attempt to extract its "message" from the whole of the experience it offers.

The artist, and perhaps especially the filmmaker, has a unique role to play in creating and sustaining the unity we seek. The techniques we employ are meant to reveal the beauty that is a form of revelation. This truth claim of art places several demands upon us, morally and spiritually, of course, but also aesthetically. Art and its techniques are wonderfully varied, but they cannot be incessantly relativized, nor should they be flattened into conformity. This is the "one size fits all" aesthetic of the mass market. Art, as a unique pursuit of truth, is inescapably hierarchical. Some art works are clearly "better," that is, more pleasing, while at the same time more truthful than others. Unfortunately, there is an approach, most evident in academia, which seems to ignore the crucial distinctions between art that is fully realized and mature, and art that is not. Christian academics too often lump Hollywood blockbusters with the best work of Kieslowski, Bresson, and Fellini as if they are all merely tools of equal value in religious and moral instruction.

Clearly, any artifact, a film or a song, can be used diagnostically in the context of a cultural anthropology; but while an egalitarian aesthetic that levels distinctions may be reassuring to some, it is profoundly discouraging for aspiring artists. It is precisely the demand to discover the means of telling the unflinching truth with compassion that challenges us to overcome "the spirit of the age." To reassure a young audience that the manufactured products of the mass media are, in their own way, as valuable as the works of artists who defy and challenge this standardized culture is to induce spiritual sleep. To allow young artists to rationalize their participation in the mechanics of mass production is to disable them creatively.

Our present search must be for the forms that most fully express our experience, thoughts, feelings, including the spiritual. This search, as

Eliot instructed, is what provokes genuine innovation and meaningful change.

I had the privilege of being instructed by two of the great pioneers in the development of the art of film — Charles Chaplin and Jean Renoir — and in my lifetime I have witnessed several revolutionary changes in film form: the neo-realists in Italy, the New Wave in France as well as the influential work of Bresson, Tarkovsky, and Kieslowski. I will attempt to offer some perspective on this legacy in the next chapter.

We ourselves may not succeed in creating the necessary new forms, but I know from experience that such changes are possible, and necessary.

PART TWO

A Brief Spiritual History of Film

The focus of this survey is on the interrelatedness of art and faith, the nexus that exists between creative exploration and spiritual need. Each filmmaker listed below responded to the spiritual needs of the time by advancing the art form, some more consciously than others. While I offer a legacy rather than a roadmap, this cinematic "genealogy" should help to place more recent innovators such as Wim Wenders, Lars von Trier, and film collaboratives such as the Dogma group and Unica in perspective.

As it is not intended to be a comprehensive history, these citations don't adequately acknowledge the influence of many significant filmmakers outside of Europe and the United States, for example, the Japanese directors Sanjiro Ozu and Akira Kurosawa, and the Indian filmmaker Satyajit Ray. This is, admittedly, a "eurocentric" orientation, because it is Euro-American culture, its inner conflicts and transformation that the history of the art of film most clearly reflects.

In the Beginning Was the Image:
Carl Dreyer and Charles Chaplin

L et's start with an "establishing long shot."
   The art of film was born in the midst of the horrors of the First World War, and developed its aesthetics during the troubled aftermath. This new art immediately reflected the rapid, often chaotic social transformations in the postwar period, including revolutions in Russia, China, and Mexico. This sense of radical change, hopeful yet threatening, can be seen in the work of the early film pioneers, particularly in Russia and Germany.

The Great Depression and the rise of totalitarian ideologies, left and right, sobered many people, as did a growing fear that another great war was inevitable. This was the spiritual context that shaped the new art.

The late 1920s also saw the climax of a sometimes exquisite silent film art, employing innovative visual story-telling techniques. The arrival of sound caused the creators of the newly voiced film dramas to be initially dependent upon theatrical skills and dramaturgy. Eventually, however, as they incorporated the silent aesthetics, these pioneers, many drawn from fields other than theater, would develop their own unique methods and explore new narrative structures.

While the early film techniques were pioneered around the world by filmmakers as diverse as Melies, Griffith, Eisenstein, Dovzhenko, Pabst, and Murnau, the art of the silent film became truly universal with the revelation of the human soul reflected in faces and eyes. At a time when mass warfare and industry were effectively denying the value of the individual person, the human face itself became a line of defense.

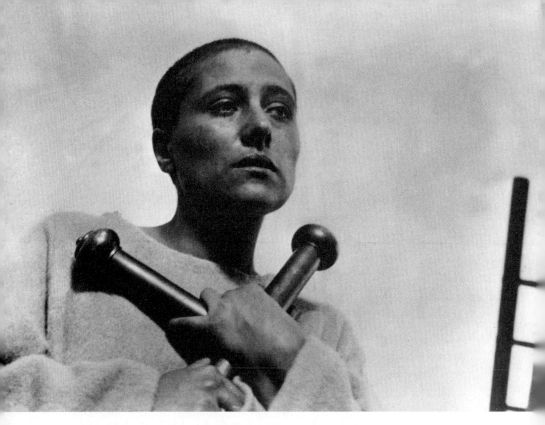

Marie Falconetti as Saint Joan in Carl Dreyer's *Passion of Joan of Arc* (1926)

CARL DREYER

Carl Dreyer's *The Passion of Joan of Arc* is a masterpiece composed of faces. Made by the distinguished Danish director with French actors in 1928, it depicts Saint Joan's trial and execution primarily in close-ups. The performance of Marie Falconetti in her only film, while displaying the theatricality of the time, is extraordinary, as is the final sequence depicting the saint's death by fire.

The film's unprecedented power was recognized at the time. In 1929, the critic of the influential *Revue du Cinema* in Paris commented that "suffering has never been shown so nakedly on the screen"; but Dreyer's theme, clear in the final montage, was that of divine grace. It remains, for many of us, the religious classic of the silent era.

Charles Chaplin in
City Lights (1931)

The development of panchromatic film in the early thirties made the close-up even more revealing and poignant.

No one demonstrated this growing capacity of the new art to move people to laughter and tears more than Charlie Chaplin.

CHARLES CHAPLIN

Chaplin's *City Lights* (1931) is, for me, his most successful feature film. *The Kid* (1921) and *The Gold Rush* (1925), his own favorite, established him as a world figure — the poor, often homeless "little chap" recognized and loved by everyone. *Modern Times*, primarily silent, though made in 1937, years after the introduction of sound, was the last of his acknowledged comedy classics.

The final matching close-ups in *City Lights*, the faces of the little tramp and the girl who is transformed by his secret love, mark one of the turning points in film history, a scene which moves audiences to tears to this day. The once-blind girl's response to the tramp's generosity — *"Yes, now I can see"* — suggests the ultimate spiritual goal of cinema itself.

Chaplin's unprecedented artistry inspired talented people throughout the world to see the potentials of cinematic art. In that later innovators such as Renoir, Welles, and Truffaut acknowledged his direct influence, Chaplin should be recognized at least as the grandfather of modern film.

The Modern Master: Jean Renoir

The French films of the 1930s, between the two world wars, were recognized for their artistry, but, understandably, displayed in the distinguished work of Marcel Carné and Jacques Prevert, for example, an
apprehensive pessimism. Yet it was in France, the battleground of the
past war and the conflagration to come, that the most eloquent and prophetic cinema voice emerged. This was Jean Renoir, the son of the great
impressionist painter, and the groundbreaking modern master of film.

Renoir's *Grand Illusion* (1937) is challenged only by his own *Rules of the
Game,* made the following year, as the masterpiece of the prewar cinema.
In *Grand Illusion* Renoir, a wounded veteran of the First World War himself, dramatizes the bravery of French prisoners of war while affirming
the humanity of their German captors, and depicts a successful escape
made possible by the unlikely friendship of a French worker, Jean Gabin,
and a Jewish prisoner played by Marcel Dalio. This was an astonishing
display of compassion, prescient of the tragedy to come, given that the
film was produced on the eve of the Second World War.

Rules of the Game is an equally powerful warning about the consequences of the cynicism and decadence hiding behind social convention.
It is the most "modern" of Renoir's films, indeed, of the period, in that it is
a self-conscious "play within a play," highly ironic, tragic, and comic, and
unblinking in its depiction of hypocrisy and social decay. Yet it remains as
compassionate in its own way as *Grand Illusion.*

Grand Illusion was recognized internationally and was the first foreign film to receive an Oscar nomination for "best picture" by the

Jean Gabin, Pierre Fresnay, and Marcel Dalio in Renoir's *Grand Illusion* (1937)

American Motion Picture Academy. *Rules of the Game*, on the other hand, was an immediate failure, denounced by French critics as "morbid," "depressing," and "immoral." It was not shown widely until after the war, by which time it was recognized in a poll of the most distinguished Hollywood directors as one of the most influential films in history.

Renoir was a genuine modern artist in that he laid bare a world of illusions, ambiguities, and lost values. These two films together capture the spiritual crisis of the time. The "grand illusion" Renoir exposes is that war can end wars; the cynical "rules" which he satirizes are of a rivalrous

Jean Renoir and Julien Carette in *Rules of the Game* (1938)

"game" that is still played, in which love is reduced to sexual conquest and possession.

To express this ironic view and the complexity of his characters, what the critic Bazin called Renoir's "hall of mirrors," the filmmaker had to further advance film technique. Renoir's use of depth of focus cinematography (aided by his cameraman brother, Claude), ensemble staging, improvisation, and inventive camera angles not only advanced the art, but anticipated further postwar innovations.

If Chaplin is the grandfather, then Jean Renoir is the *father* of modern film. A profound and loving humanist, he was a creative influence in France, a hero to the later French New Wave as well as in Italy where he inspired the young "neo-realists." Fleeing the Nazis, he came to work and teach in the United States.

I had the good fortune to attend his workshops in the postwar years, and remember his patient good humor as he advised us young film students to ignore "Hollywood" and look to the complex reality around us in the real Los Angeles.

Renoir's influence was lasting and far-reaching, and can be seen directly in Orson Welles' *Citizen Kane,* the American masterpiece of the period. Greg Toland, the film's cinematographer, advanced Renoir's deep-focus techniques, and Welles boldly created a modern antihero in Kane, whose rise and fall tore away the mask of wealth and privilege, forcing Americans to look at our own hypocrisy and corruption.

A quote of Renoir's is often cited as thematic to his compassionate work: "Everyone has his reasons."

The Search for Reality:
Vittorio De Sica and Cesare Zavattini

T he Second World War proved to be even more destructive than anyone had imagined, leaving more than thirty million dead and Europe
in ruins. In the aftermath of this tragedy, a longing for a deeper reality,
beyond both theatricality and moralism was evident in the search for
new film forms.

The most significant work immediately following the war was produced in Italy where films, primarily concerned with social justice, per-
manently altered film technique. The pioneer of Italian "neo-realism," as
it came to be called, was Roberto Rossellini, whose *Rome: Open City* and
Paisa blazed a new trail in cinematic realism through the use of non-
actors, usually with dubbed sound and actual locations. The most justly
celebrated and highly influential work of the period, however, was
achieved by a unique collaboration of an actor-director and a poet-
screenwriter.

One of the most remarkable and fruitful collaborations in cinema history, this director-writer team, Vittorio De Sica and Cesare Zavattini, created works of severe realism, but with such humanity and insight that they
changed the perspectives of film art. Their first acclaimed work was *Shoe-
shine* (1946), but it was *Bicycle Thieves* (plural, not the English mistransla-
tion "thief"), made the following year, that became the model for international filmmakers, including many then-fledgling Chinese directors.

Bicycle Thieves is more of an incident than a story. It simply depicts the
futile efforts of a poor man to recover his stolen bicycle. With this work,
De Sica brought Rossellini's approach, an interactive use of actors and

The father and son in Vittorio De Sica and Cesare Zavattini's _Bicycle Thieves_ (1947)

non-actors and actual settings, to an astonishing perfection. As Orson Welles noted, admiringly, De Sica "made the camera disappear." Zavattini's radical vision had the goal of "giving each person a name," no matter how small the part, and, under De Sica's direction, the story seemed to disappear with the camera into a vibrant, if tragic reality. The events in *Bicycle Thieves* seem insignificant, at least by Hollywood standards, and yet have provided one of the most moving and lasting film dramas.

Andre Bazin, the French film theorist, has written eloquently on the spiritual significance of the neo-realists, pointing out that the best of their work was based on a phenomenological aesthetic, in that character revelation was not psychological, but based upon "appearances and gestures." This was, as Bazin described it, a "cinema of the soul," which was not subjective, but allowed an "intuition of Being."

De Sica and Zavattini's following films, the marvelous fantasy-comedy *Miracle in Milan* and the poignant *Umberto D,* were both financial failures, yet further inspired a generation of Italian filmmakers, including Dino Risi *(Easy Life)*, Francesco Rosi *(Salvatore Guiliani)*, and the brilliant Ermmano Olmi *(Il Posto* and *Tree of the Wooden Clogs)*.

Despite its international and, indeed, historical influence, the neo-realist movement in Italy was relatively short-lived as filmmakers succumbed to the temptation of riches to be gained through sex comedies and what came to be called "spaghetti westerns." Yet another, quite singular figure emerged from its ranks. Roberto Rossellini's controversial short film *The Miracle* featured Anna Magnani, the actress most identified with the neo-realists, and, in a cameo, the film's writer briefly turned actor, Federico Fellini. By the end of the decade, Fellini, now directing his own films, succeeded in transforming the neo-realist approach into a kind of magic realism.

The Turn to the Subjective:
Federico Fellini

F ederico Fellini's work was prodigious, and over a forty-year period received international recognition. In 1993 the Academy of Motion Picture Arts and Sciences gave him a special Oscar honoring his lifetime contribution to the art of film.

However, from the very beginning, Fellini was a lightning rod for his fellow Catholics, both in Italy and abroad. In America, the Legion of Decency denounced *The Miracle*, which Fellini wrote, as "sacrilegious and blasphemous," and the attempt by the New York censors to ban the film led to a landmark Supreme Court decision that effectively ended religious censorship in the United States. The Vatican daily *L'Osservatore Romano* later condemned Fellini's *La Dolce Vita* as "disgusting" and "obscene," and some priests offered masses of atonement for viewers. Decades later, perspectives have changed. Fellini's work, now perceived as spiritually significant as well as artistically brilliant, was included in the official Vatican list of the most important films in the first hundred years of cinema.

Obviously, intent is not justification; but it is instructive to explore Fellini's intentions and his own and others' perceptions of his work. His script for the controversial *The Miracle* depicts a poor, mentally disturbed woman who, seduced by a passing stranger, becomes convinced that she has been impregnated by an angel. It was inevitable that this would offend many religious people of the time, yet, as the film's director Rossellini later explained, it was an attempt to dramatize the recognition that "God resides in everyone, especially the scorned and abandoned."

The two films that are now most often cited as evidence of Fellini's reli-

Anthony Quinn and Giulietta Masina in Federico Fellini's *La Strada* (1954)

gious sensibility are *La Strada* and, ironically, the once-condemned *La Dolce Vita*. *La Strada* (1954) starred Anthony Quinn as Zampano, a carnival strong man and Giulietta Masina as the pathetic half-witted girl whom he exploits and abandons. The theme of *La Strada* is clearly that of guilt and redemption. The ending, in which Zampano, literally at land's end, a bleak beach, faces his wasted life like a groaning animal, is ambiguous as to the possibility of redemption. Is he condemned for his cruelties, or does his painful realization of sin foretell salvation? Similarly, the ending of *La Dolce Vita* has the leading character, a disillusioned journalist (played by Fellini's celebrated *alter ego* Marcello Mastroianni) wandering on a beach after a night of debauchery. Again, there is an uncertain note of redemption. The journalist observes a one-eyed sea monster, a freak of nature that has washed ashore, a fairly obvious symbol of his own estrangement, and then watches as an innocent young girl (Fellini's symbols of innocence and grace are invariably young and poor) tries to summon him to join her from a seemingly unbridgeable distance. He cannot understand her appeals and turns away. A hint of grace, or simply a memory of a lost childhood? It is open to interpretation, but Fellini himself claimed that *La Dolce Vita* was "a profoundly Christian film."

Perhaps what offended so many Italian Catholics was Fellini's relentless satire of a corrupt postwar world in which they were implicated, which they tolerated. Commenting on his film adaptation of Petronius's *Satyricon*, depicting the decadence of ancient Rome, Fellini observed that "Rome in its decline is quite similar to our world today. . . . [T]he same fury of enjoying life, the same lack of moral principles."

Pier Paolo Pasolini, a highly controversial filmmaker himself, the creator of the remarkable *The Gospel According to Matthew*, criticized Fellini as a "naive and infantile Catholic" because Fellini saw the world as "regulated by Grace" — hardly a judgment that will be sustained by most Catholics. Yet the essentially nonreligious Pasolini recognized the "loving and sympathetic optimism" in Fellini's films, which, Pasolini concluded, "overflow with undifferentiated love."

One can see in Fellini's best work the influence of Chaplin, particularly in the marvelous performances of his wife Giulietta Masina in *La Strada* and the later *Nights of Cabiria*. His kinship to Renoir is apparent in that they share an uncompromising look at moral corruption tempered with a great love for humanity.

There is a highly modern "turn to the subjective" in much of Fellini's later work, such as the erratic *Giulietta of the Spirits*. The extreme subjectivity, a mixing of dreams and wakefulness, desire and illusion in *8½ (Otto e Mezzo,* 1962) makes it a landmark film of contemporary sensibility. The illusory, narcissistic world of the filmmaker, probably uncomfortably close to Fellini's own life, captures an accelerating trend in modern life, hardly limited to the movies. The filmmaker Guido, portrayed again by Mastroianni, is unable to continue his work, paralyzed by self-doubt and guilt induced by his infidelities. The title indicates his sense of incompletion in that only a "half" of a film now seems possible.

The characters portrayed by Marcello Mastroianni in Fellini's films, such as the young journalist in *La Dolce Vita*, seem to be inwardly dying,

Marcello Mastroianni in Fellini's _La Dolce Vita_ (1960)

torn apart by an irreconcilable awareness of a desire beyond illusion and an incapacity to love faithfully.

   Fellini's huge success undoubtedly disconnected him to some degree from his religious roots. Fellini's "Catholic" perspective can also be criticized as a simplistic reduction of the Gospels to a vague humanitarianism. Fellini may be, with the rest of us, a product of the decadence of the times that he morally condemns; but, especially in his earlier films, he is not despairing and seems to recognize, with St. Paul, that "where there is evil, grace abounds."

"Be Attentive":
The Films of Robert Bresson

At the same time that Italy was witnessing a film renaissance, not always appreciated by the Italians themselves, yet another singular figure emerged again in France.

The most provocative, if not difficult, filmmaker of modern times, Robert Bresson created profoundly spiritual work that attempted to radically purify film form, and the challenge of his legacy remains to this day.

An old friend, the late Pauline Kael, the most noted film critic of my generation, was no friend of religious sentiment. It was a prejudice that I fear made her and many of my contemporaries spiritually color-blind; yet Pauline recognized the power in at least one of the films of Robert Bresson. Retrospectively reviewing his *Diary of a Country Priest* made in 1950, Pauline commended it for its "great purity," which recognized Bresson's aesthetic goal and "its Bach-like intensity." The film, she continued, was "one of the few modern works in any art form that helps one to understand the religious life."

One of the spiritual masters of cinema, Bresson's gradual development of a "pure" form through the discipline of attention can be seen in his three now-classic films: *Diary of a Country Priest, A Man Condemned to Death Escapes,* and *Pickpocket.*

While *Diary of a Country Priest,* adapted from the Bernanos novel, remains powerful, and the subsequent film *Pickpocket* perhaps most fulfills Bresson's extreme aesthetic goals, I believe *A Man Condemned to Death Escapes* is his most successful work.

A Man Condemned to Death Escapes is sometimes re-titled in English *A*

The prisoner in Robert Bresson's *A Man Condemned to Death Escapes* (1956)

Man Escaped, but the full title, even longer, contains the biblical phrase "where the wind bloweth," revealing the work's spiritual roots and aim. The depiction, hardly a story, and mostly silent with minimal music, is of a French resistance fighter's escape from German execution. Based on a true account, it is rendered, however, into a kind of visual poetry in which inanimate objects as well as human faces assume metaphysical significance. The film's austerity, so extreme that some critics considered it perverse, doesn't repress but enhances the sense of liberation we feel at the end. Somehow, on some level, we "escape" with the condemned man.

In his sometimes cryptic published notebooks, Bresson, nonetheless, clearly stated his objectives and methodology as being based on what I've called being in the present moment. Bresson's own words are similar to the directive in the Eastern Catholic liturgy: "Be attentive!"

Bresson rejected most of cinema as "a school of inattention in which we look without seeing." He urged filmmakers to "build your film on white, on silence, and on stillness." This was a severe aesthetic without recourse to theatrics. Bresson refused to "draw tears with tears," and saw films as ineffectual if they were "an art conceived in another art's form" — in other words, derivative of theater or literature. For many filmmakers around the world, his work succeeded and inspired new impulses. Andre Bazin, always so astute, wrote that "in the faces of Bresson, we look not for fleeting reflections but for the soul," an expression suggesting the future path of Kieslowski, among others.

The difficulty we have in appreciating, or even understanding, Bresson's films comes from the danger of being exposed to so many images in daily life. We need fresh eyes to follow his search for truth in a pure form. One might describe him as an iconographer who, in that great tradition, aspires to create images that "express through compression." The challenge in making films, Bresson understood, was in creating an inner discipline. His ultimate advice was to "provoke the unexpected. Expect it!"

Bresson's later work, beginning with *Au Hazard Balthasar*, turned grimly pessimistic, if not Jansenist (the heretical but persistent tendency to deny the goodness of creation). His spiritual search, however, made him the most truly avant-garde filmmaker in film history.

The Age of Anxiety:
The Films of Ingmar Bergman

I n postwar Europe, its bombed-out ruins still under repair, "history" was no longer the inspiring sweep of Napoleon's conquests or Marx's dream of revolution. As Joyce's Stephen Daedalus described it a generation earlier, history had become "a nightmare from which I'm trying to escape."

Poet W. H. Auden termed the postwar years of the 1950's the "age of anxiety." This sense of peril wasn't simply due to the onset of the cold war and the risk of nuclear catastrophe; it reflected a deeper sense of disconnectedness. No one dissected this modern condition more relentlessly than a contemporary of Bresson and Fellini's, the Swedish director Ingmar Bergman.

Born in 1918, the son of a clergyman, Ingmar Bergman was a distinguished director at the Royal Theater in Stockholm who staged outstanding productions of Shakespeare, Ibsen, and contemporary drama. He would demonstrate his theatrical gifts throughout his film work, including a memorable film version of Mozart's *Magic Flute*. In 1955, he received recognition for his film *Smiles of a Summer Night*, and subsequently created a body of intense and often quite personal films that would be influential throughout the world.

While international acclaim greeted his imaginative religious dramas *The Seventh Seal* and *Virgin Spring*, I consider *Wild Strawberries*, made in 1957, Bergman's most significant film. The central character, a retired doctor, Isak, played by Victor Sjostrom, looks back at his life with all its losses. Bergman blends dream-like memories with a cold, unfulfilled pres-

Victor Sjoberg and Bibi Andersson in Ingmar Bergman's *Wild Strawberries* (1957)

ent. Older and even more despairing than Fellini's Guido in *8½*, Isak now realizes that he has led a false, largely loveless life, filled with self-deception. Again, we are being offered a deeply spiritual insight into the falsity of modern life and its functional, self-satisfying rather than self-sacrificing relationships.

Made at the end of Bergman's career, *Fannie and Alexander* is in the best humanist tradition, universal in its sympathetic look at family members tormented by loss and regret, yet still capable of a forgiving embrace. This may reflect Bergman's personal life, marked by a series of broken relationships; and his spiritual search, relentlessly despairing, was undoubtedly spurred by these losses. In seeking formal expression, this search produced an austere style and, aided by his collaboration with the talented cinematographer Sven Nykvist, produced at times a true visual poetry.

Bergman was, nonetheless, primarily a man of the theater. Much of his finest work is distinguished by the remarkable performances he elicited from actors such as Sjostrom (himself a director), Max von Sydow, Liv Ullmann, and Bibi Andersson. It is this theatrical orientation, the tendency to create "performance" rather than simply "presence" that, in my judgment, limits Bergman's otherwise remarkable work. In contrast to De Sica's self-effacing approach or, most certainly, to Bresson's vision, Bergman remains more rooted in a theatrical tradition than the others, yet his talent was such that his work enlarged the cinematic imagination.

A "New Wave" in France:
Eric Rohmer and François Truffaut

S imultaneous with the best work of Fellini and Bergman, the young French filmmakers known by the label *nouvelle vague*, or New Wave, broke truly new ground in content and form. With an unprecedented approach to narrative continuity or, sometimes, discontinuity, these films reflected the growing social displacement of urban youth everywhere and their angry rejection of past literary and social traditions.

While highly individual, their work had common ground in its origins, the ideas and inspiration of Andre Bazin, a Catholic personalist and the leading film theoretician of the time. The New Wave began as an expression of youthful alienation, embodied in the quasi-criminal characters in films such as Godard's *Breathless*, somewhat pretentious and over-praised at the time, but the first to achieve international recognition. This New Wave included filmmakers who would evolve quite distinct and personal styles, including Jean-Luc Godard, Claude Chabrol, and Louis Malle.

Despite the issuing of a "manifesto" proclaiming principles inspired by the Italian neo-realists, the New Wave was more of an alliance of rebels than a movement adhering to any ideology. In fact, two of the most distinctive members of the group, the two whose work, in my opinion, will endure, are strikingly different in many ways. They are Eric Rohmer and François Truffaut.

ERIC ROHMER

The oldest in age and, seemingly, the least adventuresome of the group in exploring new forms, Eric Rohmer, whose real name was Jean-Marie Scherer, offers us what are apparently little more than filmed conversations. Yet his thoughtful work, with its subtle insights into human frailties, may prove to be the most lasting in what it reveals of the spiritual conditions of the time.

Rohmer's *Moral Tales*, a series of six films, are more in the French literary tradition than they are overtly religious. His most noted, as well as successful, film in this series was *My Night at Maud's* made in 1969.

A deceptively simple story of a young man who resists the seductive enticements of a sophisticated woman, Maud, and who then finds — in church, no less — his future wife, the film was an inexplicable commercial and critical success in France and abroad. Looking back more than a quarter of a century later, perhaps we can sense why. There were cries for radical change, indeed, revolution, in the streets of Paris in those years. In fact, the turbulent events that occurred in Paris in 1968 came to be described as the "days of rage." In addition to the political turmoil, the counterculture was already taking its toll on moral norms in the name of "liberation." However, an emptiness, a spiritual vacuum, so wonderfully captured in Rohmer's films was already being felt. I think audiences, including urban sophisticates, responded intuitively to Rohmer's "counterrevolutionary" defense of traditional morality. In France, typically and sadly, the critics divided into left and right camps, more or less liberationists versus Catholics, yet there was general agreement as to Rohmer's artistry and integrity.

One French critic described *My Night at Maud's* as a "chamber movie" because of his daringly confined scale, with so much of the talk taking place in Maud's small apartment. Others saw it as a cinematic fulfillment of the philosophical *moraliste* tradition of Pascal, often quoted in the dialogue, and poet Paul Valery. Another critical comment, in praise of the film, sums up a characteristic not only of Rohmer's work, but also of the body of films that I've cited. Rather that offering merely entertainment, the film "demands the attention and participation of the audience."

In retrospect, Rohmer's own comments reveal more, I believe, about his aesthetics and how they relate to his beliefs. In his preface to the published scripts of the *Moral Tales,* Rohmer describes his approach as offering an "account" of events rather that a direct depiction of the events themselves. It is the interior life of the central character, not merely his subjective disposition, but the arena of will and choice that he tries to present, thus providing "a moral tale." Much of this interiority was originally conveyed in first-person narration, but Rohmer notes that a good deal of this was then rendered into dialogue. Yet the dialogue itself is often an "account," a story of past actions, reflecting the character's desires and his crisis of conscience.

This approach, so dependent upon dialogue, is what makes *My Night at Maud's,* or the film that followed, *Chloe in the Afternoon,* seem more conventional, even mistaken for "old-fashioned." In his own quiet way, Rohmer's approach was as revolutionary as Godard's, or any of the others. The technique is, of course, far less improvisational than that of many of his New Wave contemporaries; but Rohmer stresses that the camera and actors were transforming agents, and that the ultimate story and its meaning is on the screen. The process of filming, Rohmer relates, disabuses one of the notion that the characters, or the filmmaker himself, are omniscient.

At times, the relentless intellectualizing of emotion can distance us, but there is an underlying compassion in Rohmer's work. His seductresses, Maud and Chloe, are not only fully drawn, indeed, entrancing characters, but each has suffered deeply. Maud lost her one true love in a car accident and Chloe openly reveals her despair and loneliness.

According to Rohmer, his mentor Bazin's central idea was to affirm the revelation that comes from "the objectivity of the cinema" as opposed to subjectivism and theatrical manipulation.

It was described as an approach "obligated to God and the reality of the universe." We can see the affinities with Bresson and the neo-realists here. However, Rohmer's approach was to capture this ontological reality in long uninterrupted takes. It is, again, an anti-psychological aesthetic that folds individuals into a greater reality than their own personal histories. Rohmer's approach affirms, quite clearly, I believe, the essential Thomistic idea of love as "affirmation of Being," which, in cinema can be simply the "joy of recognition."

Zouzou in Eric Rohmer's *Chloe in the Afternoon* (1972)

These aesthetic strategies, from Fellini to Rohmer, while clearly diverse, are all attempts to find a meaning in life that is essentially religious in character. The "religious" dimension means exploring the fullness of psychological and sociological reality while, at the same time, opening the audience to the experience of the sacred.

In doing this, however, Rohmer, following Bazin's admonitions, disallows any attempt at the physical representation of Grace or the supernatural, but pursues the transcendent through a strict, almost prosaic naturalism.

Rohmer's *Six Moral Tales* include *Claire's Knee* and *Chloe in the Afternoon*, the last of the series made in 1972, all dealing with the themes of temptation and redemption. The *Tales* were then followed by his *Comedies and Proverbs*, which continued, with gentle humor and insight, to contrast the French mythologies of sex with moral and psychological reality.

FRANÇOIS TRUFFAUT

Andre Bazin's closest disciple, indeed, almost an adopted son, François Truffaut became the best known of the New Wave group, and, in many ways, its leader. He initially followed in Bazin's footsteps as a critic, and then, achieving success as a filmmaker, helped the others, artistically and financially. I believe his films artfully synthesize the New Wave legacy, the humanist tradition of Renoir with their collective rebellious imagination.

In the tradition of Renoir, yet devoted to Hitchcock's cinematic "bag of tricks" and Hollywood *noir* gangster films, Truffaut's work is eclectic and uneven; but it includes some modern masterworks, such as *Four Hundred Blows, Jules et Jim,* and probably the best film ever made about filmmaking, *Day for Night.*

As a critic loyal to Bazin's vision, Truffaut championed the lyricism of the films of Renoir and an earlier pioneer, Jean Vigo. He so ferociously rejected the politico-literary status quo that, as a film critic, he was termed "the gravedigger of the French cinema."

The 1958 New Wave manifesto declared that their films, in contrast to highly polished studio products, would be more spontaneous personal works. The so-called *auteur* theory would rise out of this early dedication to a personal vision, unsubordinated to any literary source, or even a rigidly pre-planned script. Some film directors would later appropriate the *auteur* theory for their own often-shameless self-promotion. The New Wave goal, however, was to sustain a single unified vision, uncompromised by Hollywood studio practices that often pit writer against director.

While breaking with the immediate past, Truffaut was still nourished by older traditions, philosophical and religious. Inspired by Pascal's *Pensees,* in 1951 he wrote "fifteen aphorisms on cinema" which he gave to his mentor, Bazin, and Eric Rohmer. In 1955 Truffaut and Rohmer worked together on a screenplay about "the modern church," which was never produced.

Jean-Pierre Leaud in François Truffaut's *Four Hundred Blows* (1958)

Nevertheless, in an essential way, Truffaut was to remain an *enfant terrible* throughout his life and career. Once confined as a juvenile offender himself, he strongly identified with the increasing number of young people emotionally displaced by the breakdown of the family and social norms. Some of his best films are about children, including *The Wild Child* and *Small Change,* and they remain fresh and remarkable.

Four Hundred Blows (1958) is Truffaut's signature work. It was the first of five, vaguely autobiographical films made over twenty years, all starring Jean-Pierre Leaud, who became Truffaut's cinematic *alter-ego.* A heart-breaking story, *Four Hundred Blows* depicts an emotionally abandoned child who, fleeing from all adult authority, ends up desperately alone, literally at the edge of the sea.

In the remaining films of the series, we witness the boy-turned-man's futile attempt to find lasting love and security. Antoine never quite grows up, and his love affairs and even marriage seem child-like in their hopeful innocence and lack of reality. Truffaut came to believe that the "couple solution," whether in marriage or outside of it, fails to sustain love; but then concludes, with an honesty that anticipates Woody Allen, neither do any of the sexual "experiments in freedom."

Jules et Jim (1961), acclaimed at the time for its boldness, further established Truffaut's international reputation. The story of an ill-fated *menage a trois*, it featured actress Jeanne Moreau as a totally "free" but self-absorbed woman who "invents her life at every moment." She and her two lovers are torn apart, emotionally and physically, and finally united only in death.

In retrospect, although it anticipated much to come, *Jules et Jim*, with its preoccupation with sexual freedom, now seems particularly representative of the conflicted attitudes of the sixties. It has been described as a "hymn to absolute freedom in love — and its impossibility." These sexual pioneers now seem as emotionally trapped as anyone caught in a suffocating marriage.

Truffaut's creative relationships with his New Wave colleagues, such as Rohmer and Godard and with the actor Jean-Pierre Leaud, provide yet another example of the essentially collaborative process of filmmaking. Despite the refusal to be confined by a script, Truffaut was in some ways more dedicated to language than images, and also elicited the collaboration of talented writers such as Marcel Moussy, Jean-Louis Richard, and Suzanne Schiffman. The manner of Truffaut's collaboration with other writers was, however, a far cry from Hollywood's territorial defense process. For one thing, the initial scripts were seldom more than synopses based on events often drawn from memory, with the essential dialogue remaining in Truffaut's head. I remember Renoir recommending a similar approach that he called the "Italian method," in which the actors would be discouraged from too much interpretation or expressed emotion in rehearsal so as to preserve the spontaneity and possible surprises for the actual moments of filming.

François Truffaut died at age fifty-two in 1984. His early death deprived us of what might have been yet another stage of his rich inventive work. His next film would have been a female version of *Four Hundred Blows.*

To describe Truffaut's work as "spiritual" is not to suggest that it necessarily manifested any religious belief. It has been said that "Truffaut's religion was Charlie Chaplin." He had no particular interest in philosophy and, like Chaplin, was self-educated — in Truffaut's case, primarily through movies. As with so many of my contemporaries, movies, or art in general, were seen as the source of redemption. Given his frustrated search for an enduring love, it is understandable that Truffaut was tempted to retreat into a "B" movie world where death can literally become a joke. This was the magic world of Hollywood entertainment he discovered during his youth, a time of shame and degradation for his defeated countrymen. It was an understandable retreat, and we can only be grateful that he did not fully succumb to it.

My inclusion of Truffaut into this spiritual chronology is not, however, merely a tribute to his honesty or artistry. I perceive a direct line, an "arc," from his work of a half-century ago to the present. It is my experience, working with young filmmakers, that relationships, particularly sexual ones, are now their "spiritual arena." Transcendence is to be sought, somehow, in the other person, the beloved, or, at least, the possessed, if only momentarily. I believe Truffaut anticipates a certain inevitability in this tendency. Despite the desired goal of merging with the Other, lacking a transcendent source of love, these relationships become, inexorably, not lasting love but a *folie a deux*, or just another subjective trap.

The influence of the French New Wave was widespread, and, at the time, struck American film students, such as myself, as an irreversible revolution. The domination of the classic Hollywood style with its seamless camerawork, smooth transitions, and clear exposition was over. Young filmmakers were ready to take increasing risks, and audiences came to accept this new vocabulary.

The "New Hollywood":
Martin Scorsese and Woody Allen

In America, the counterculture of the sixties and seventies sprang from a youthful idealism thwarted not just by external power, but by its own fundamental contradictions. Primarily a student protest among the educated and privileged, it was made possible by the affluence and materialism that, however briefly, it sought to reject. After a few years of genuine commitment to racial equality and concern for the poor, the "movement" collapsed into the indulgences of drugs, sex, and the political theater of violent gestures of futility.

It was not the original idealism, but the aftermath of profound disillusionment that provided the media content of the era to follow. This was evident in *Easy Rider* (1969), an indulgent and self-pitying portrayal of "rebels" in which even a superficial nonconformity provokes irrational murder. This estrangement of the young, a worldwide phenomenon of the late sixties, had been anticipated earlier by "beat" poets and "cool" jazz, and, in America, by the films of Stanley Kubrick. His *Doctor Strangelove; or, How I Learned to Love the Bomb* (1963) was a landmark of ferocious black comedy about the then-anticipated horror of mass destruction. Kubrick's later *2001: A Space Odyssey*, written by the science popularizer Arthur Clarke, was an imaginative attempt to merge anthropology, technology, and metaphysical inquiry without recourse to religious tradition. Significantly, given the American obsession with technology, the futuristic technological advances in *2001* are perceived, as in *Dr. Strangelove*, as more threatening, even nightmarish, than curative or hopeful.

Throughout the sixties, the most successful Hollywood films were those which still offered the light fare for which the industry was justly famous — *My Fair Lady, Mary Poppins,* the *Pink Panther* series, and, in 1965, the blockbuster *Sound of Music.* However, a dark pessimism unlike the socially conscious, prewar *noir* films was becoming evident as early as 1967 in the skillful, but nihilistic *Bonnie and Clyde.* I remember after a Writers Guild screening of this film, a distinguished older screenwriter remarked with sad puzzlement: "We used to give the public their dreams; now we give them their nightmares." It is not a criticism, or a disregard for the honesty or the artistry involved, to note this trend. Many of the most talented filmmakers in Hollywood were increasingly attune to what was happening in the culture and tried to portray it in films such as *The Graduate, In Cold Blood,* and, in 1969, the Oscar-winning *Midnight Cowboy.*

The spiritual malaise evident in American films during the 1970s has been attributed to various causes, such as the assassinations of Kennedy and King, and disunity caused by the war in Vietnam. Yet, as we've noted, the rebellious disaffection of youth in the late sixties was worldwide, creating near anarchy in France and China and prolonged violence in Germany, Italy, and Mexico. There were obviously deeper causes, suggesting that the malaise was more spiritual than political.

The new generation of American filmmakers in the seventies had been weaned on the visual techniques of film and television, and now merged American technological know-how with the aesthetic advances of the Europeans and Japanese. As the work of these new filmmakers, many of them the first graduates of film schools, became successful, there was much talk of a "new Hollywood" liberated from the commercial restrictions of the past. This proved to be somewhat premature, because by the end of the decade, some of these same filmmakers, such as Lucas and Spielberg, would be using "old Hollywood" approaches to entertainment to woo back disaffected audiences.

Nonetheless, the most significant films of the era would expose, if not necessarily comprehend the spiritual crisis of the time. They include Francis Ford Coppola's award-winning *Godfather* films (1971-72), and his often powerful, though tellingly incoherent, *Apocalypse Now.* Also notable were Roman Polanski and writer Robert Towne's *Chinatown* (1974) and *One Flew Over the Cuckoo's Nest,* directed by the talented Czech filmmaker Milos Forman and voted the "best picture" of 1975 by the Academy.

Al Pacino in Francis Ford Coppola's *Godfather II* (1973)

In the late seventies, something significantly "new" did emerge. The first films of the two most influential American filmmakers of the time appeared. These were Martin Scorsese's production of *Taxi Driver* (1976) and Woody Allen's *Annie Hall*, the Academy's "best picture" of 1977.

MARTIN SCORSESE

Martin Scorsese may indeed prove be the great filmmaker who never made a great film. Orson Welles, the first to be so described, at least created *Citizen Kane*. This is a judgment that will be disputed, of course, by the many admirers of Scorsese's films, particularly *Taxi Driver* and *Raging Bull*. I doubt that there are many who still persist in admiring *Last Temptation of Christ* for anything but Scorsese's tenacity in getting it made. *Last Temptation* has effective moments, but doesn't cohere aesthetically, the awkward dialogue occasionally provoking audience laughter. Much of Scorsese's other work, such as *Goodfellas*, with its dazzling camera work, seems as spiritually empty as its characters. Even the brilliantly directed *Kandun*, depicting the early life of the Dalai Lama, lacks a spiritual conviction comparable to its occasionally inspired imagery.

A former Catholic seminarian, Scorsese's claim that, for him, religion and film are the most, if not only, important matters in his life marks not only his own distinction, but perhaps a new sensibility among American filmmakers. However, to my eyes, Scorsese never seems to be able to successfully merge his two central concerns. There are many hard truths in Scorsese's films, but seldom a deep compassion or hint of redemption, and, hence, little hope. This limitation clearly does not stem from a lack of talent, for Scorsese is a modern master of technique.

This, I believe, is instructive in itself. To what extent does a preoccupation with form and technique become an impediment, even a substitute for insight, and, to use a much-abused word, authenticity? I've encountered numerous young Christians and people of other faiths, unquestionably sincere and spiritually mature, whose lack of technique or talent prevents them from finding the expressive forms they seek. This is, sadly, commonplace. But is there not a corresponding danger, though less common, that a talent overly preoccupied with technique and artfulness might lead to merely "making movies about movies"? I remember that Jean Renoir recognized this danger, and warned us young Americans that our obsession with perfecting technique was our cultural weakness.

My deeper concern, however, goes beyond form and technique. The "magic of movies," even if incorporating traditional imagery, can easily distort religious experience. This is as true of the Hollywood biblical spectacles, with their special effects "miracles," as it is of the sometimes mocking imagery of Buñuel or Altman. No one is redeemed by a movie, no matter the quality or intent. As Malcolm Muggeridge once said, "Jesus came in the flesh, not celluloid."

Neither can the movies provide a substitute for religious faith. Terence Davies, a talented British filmmaker whose *Distant Voices, Private Lives* is painfully honest and boldly inventive, acknowledges that his rejection of his working class family's Catholicism motivated his filmmaking. Davies sees only "chaos beneath heaven," and makes films as a means of controlling the effects of that chaos. Davies depicts the sad and indeed brutal aspects of his family life, but I believe that this temptation to replace the iconography of traditional belief with one's own private imagery goes beyond personal grievances. Whatever wounds religion might inflict, the temptation to exalt one's own mirror reflections instead is as perennial and futile as the invention of the golden calf. What young filmmakers, many now seeking faith, but without tradition, should note is the spiritual emptiness so clearly evident in these surrogate devotions.

However this might pertain to Scorsese, and whether my judgment of the cohesiveness of his work is fair or not, Scorsese's finely crafted films are inspiring to many, and his grim vision of late twentieth century America will undoubtedly remain a valuable part of our legacy.

WOODY ALLEN

If filmmakers of religious belief had the integrity and courage of Woody Allen's disbelief, we would have a renaissance of films of faith. But, of course, we would need his talent as well.

The best of his parochial, but brilliant comedies — *Annie Hall, Hannah and Her Sisters,* and *Crimes and Misdemeanors* — mirror the disillusionment-turning-to-despair of a generation of urban sophisticates. While rendering it into sometimes broad comedy, Allen seldom compromises the truth, especially about himself and his cultural constituency.

For me, *Crimes and Misdemeanors* is his most remarkable work, an artful blend of near-farce with virtual tragedy. Whether this unique composite technique, a very modern pastiche of stand-up comedy, monologue, and visual jokes, amounts to a legacy is uncertain, but it is a form that arises from the distinctly American tradition of fruitfully merging "high" and "low" cultures.

Woody Allen is a modern Jewish prophet who, from the perspective of traditional Jews and Christians, has lost his way in the spiritual desert of fashionable Manhattan. But, faithful to the anti-idolatrous Jewish tradition, he refuses to offer any substitute for God — not "religion," or politics, or psychotherapy, all of which Allen lampoons, sometimes unfairly. Ultimately, his last hope, grasping at sexual intimacy as a form of self-transcendence, proves to be only a briefly comforting illusion. "Life is

Martin Landau and Woody Allen in Allen's *Crimes and Misdemeanors* (1988)

only meaningful when there is a God," proclaimeth Woody, "and there is no God." It is, clearly, a very sad situation; yet, as Charlie Chaplin said, "Once something is too tragic, it becomes funny."

Woody Allen's comedy, hilarious yet rooted in hopelessness, is so utterly self-conscious that it becomes a parody of modern subjectivity. It is not, however, the God of Moses or Jesus who dies in Allen's satire — this God is already absent. What we lament in Allen's work is the death of Venus, the "gradual but inevitable cooling of bodies." In this respect, Allen is akin to both Bergman, one of his heroes, and to Truffaut, his contemporary, in their exposure of the sad pretenses of romantic love.

There is, I believe, a greater significance to be found in what may seem at times trivial comedy. The comedy genre has often been the most insightful in American film. I would suggest that to appreciate the bitterly critical comedy of Woody Allen requires all those qualities to which Christians hopefully aspire: humility, the confession of guilt, forgiveness, and, of course, a sense of humor. His work also illuminates a contemporary Jewish sensibility that is highly influential in popular culture, and worth our serious examination.

To best understand a Jewish attitude, we should first turn to Jewish sources. The writings of Franz Rosenzweig, one of the most respected Jewish philosophers of the twentieth century, suggest a relationship between Judaism and art that, I believe, at least partially explains Woody's despair.

Rosenzweig considered what he called the "magic flute of art" to be an attempt to create "the only eternity available" to us; but it does so at the price of "isolation and self-containedness." In creating art, perhaps especially movies, we create a world of make-believe, a "world of mere possibility" in which, Rosenzweig observed, the "Self remains behind walls."

Rosenzweig related this central aspect of art to Judaism itself. As with the highest art, it is the mission of Judaism to provide a profound shock, a form of attention that forces us to confront the need for personal transformation. Jews are the "people of the Book" who speak their own language, traditionally a language of signs and miracles as much as words, hence its universality. The price for speaking these words, for administering this shock, has been a perpetual homelessness. The role of Jews in culture is always a state of being simultaneously the elect and the outcast, greeted with both blessings and curses.

The Greek tradition, which Judaism challenged, now reemerging as modern neo-stoicism, knew that death could not be comprehended and saw the recognition of finitude as wisdom. But Judaism, again, as with high art, responds to death with a sense of the uncanny, the recognition of some living force beyond personal finitude. This is what Allen, following Freud, dismisses as "magical thinking." This is an ironic criticism, considering that movies, more than religion, now provide our imagined world. If "magical thinking" means a narcissistic evasion of reality, then, in my experience, present-day Hollywood is the world capital of magical thought.

The despair in Woody Allen isn't significantly different than that found in Isaiah, or, for that matter, Dante. It is hardly a "modern" product, but part of a dialectic that is as old as Judaism and abounds in the Psalms. It's a shame that Woody didn't have a chance to meet Jeremiah.

The vision that art offers, however despairing in itself, produces an essential human commonality that does not deny the suffering of others. The Christian recognition of unjust suffering and death — the finitude embodied, literally, on the Cross — creates our community. It is the prerequisite not only for community, but for redemption.

What troubles Christians about Woody Allen may not be so much his "disbelief" — possibly more his problem than ours, but the inherent challenge that Franz Rosenzweig saw in Judaism's response to Christianity. Judaism denies that Christianity has fulfilled its mission. Most particularly, it rejects the idea that the Messiah has arrived, whether Jesus or anyone else, given the evidence of an unredeemed world. Christians have a different understanding, of course, but it remains the Jewish mission to challenge the Christian temptation to self-justification and idolatry. Jews did this historically simply by being a presence, an offense in itself to a self-doubting Christian. Art, if it is courageous and truthful, does the same.

Jews, whether Jeremiah confronting his own people, Franz Rosenzweig and Martin Buber challenging the worldly status quo, or a funny little New York comedian, must always be taken seriously when they speak to us in these terms. It is the role that God has given them, even if they think they're only speaking for themselves.

The Age of Miracles:
Andrei Tarkovsky and Krzysztof Kieslowski

As hope for radical social change receded and Hollywood's new generation turned increasingly to the formulas of the past, including rounds of endless remakes, cynicism became as fashionable in the industry as designer drugs.

By the 1980s, the media, including films, and the so-called "youth culture" had become virtually synonymous. American wealth had provided unprecedented disposable income for minors, and the style and content of films now reflected this targeted market. Increasingly young and capricious, the attention span of media consumers now demanded rapid-fire imagery and high-decibel noise. Studio executives, in turn, required filmmakers to cram the "product," as it was now commonly called, with artificial emotional stimulants, whether naked flesh or car explosions — what one of the early youth market producers called "wham-o's."

Outside of Hollywood, however, two cinematic miracles took place that renewed our spirits and, in time, became the most influential creative forces in the film world. The two miracles were named Andrei Tarkovsky and Krzysztof Kieslowski.

In addition to the difficulty of their names, these two unlikely "miracles" had much in common. Both were Slavs — one Russian, the other Polish — exiles from Communism, and deeply concerned with religious questions. Indeed, the openly spiritual content of their films necessitated their seeking freedom elsewhere. Tarkovsky fled to Sweden from the atheist strictures of the moribund Soviet Union; Kieslowski departed the failing communist regime in Poland to work in France. They also suffered untimely deaths, depriving us of the possibility of even greater work.

Andrei Tarkovsky

With Bresson, Tarkovsky is one of the most uncompromising explorers of the spiritual depth of film. As such, his films can be difficult to penetrate. His work preceded that of Kieslowski, but became even more widely influential in the decade after his death in 1986.

His films are very "Russian," some painfully long and digressive by contemporary media standards. They seem as "perverse" at times as Bresson's, as if indifferent to audience comfort, much less demands for entertainment. One of the games played at the commissary "writers' table" by the screenwriters of my generation was to imagine "pitching" one of, say, Fellini's or Bergman's films to a studio executive. The consequence would have been immediate unemployment. To "pitch" a Tarkovsky film would have meant risking hospitalization.

His acknowledged masterpiece is *Andrei Rublev*, depicting the struggles of the great seventeenth-century Russian icon painter. It is an extraordinary cinematic canvas of haunting images. On more than one occasion, I have seen American film students left in a state of awe and admiration by this work.

The Sacrifice, made in Sweden, evokes our collective fears of mass destruction. Tarkovsky's seminal thoughts and dogged determination in making this film are caught in Michal Leszczylowski's documentary *Directed by Andrei Tarkovsky*. His "science fiction" film *Solaris*, made in Russia in 1972, has achieved a kind of cult status, and has had the dubious distinction of being remade in Hollywood. The original was made on a fraction of a Hollywood budget, relying on the force of Tarkovsky's extraordinary imagination and meditative intelligence. It raises serious questions about the survival of what is human in a technologically perfected future.

However, in my opinion, the most challenging and exciting work, in its exploration of the potential of film form, is *Mirror*. Baffling initially even to his fellow Russians, *Mirror* moves even further beyond conventional

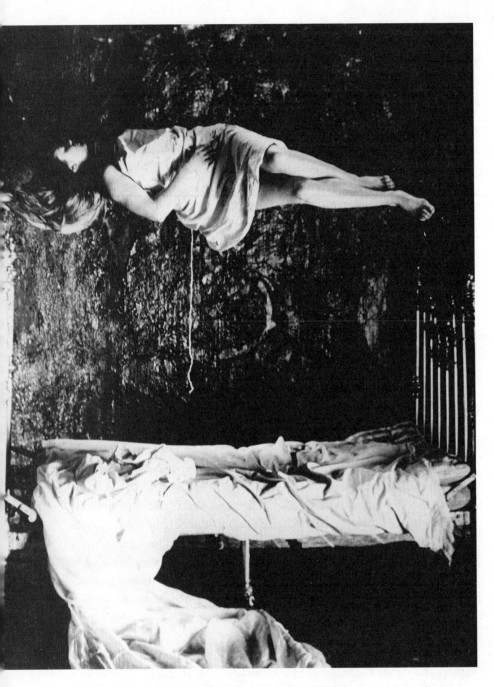

The "floating woman" in Andrei Tarkovski's *Mirror* (1974)

narrative to a poetic evocation of life and death as experienced in the mind of an apparently dying man. As with the best of poetry or music, the film seldom reveals itself in one viewing; but in its astonishing blend of word and image, present time and memory, it opens new doors to a form of cinematic poetry.

Tarkovsky's work, not emotionally restricted as with Bresson, provides the best example of the unique potential of film as an autonomous art, dependent upon neither theater nor literature. What I mean by the "theatrical" in films, as I have applied the term to the later Fellini, most of Bergman, or many fine Hollywood films, is not simply the use of the methodology and techniques of the theater, but an attitude toward the audience. Theater provides its own great art but, on film, it becomes "life on stilts," that is, bigger than life. The goal of the film artist is to simply stand on one's feet, eye to eye with the viewer. A theatrical film is "about" something. The films that I believe advance the art simply "are." The credo of such a filmmaker should be: "I am concealing nothing from you because I have no designs on you. I have nothing to teach you. I am simply one in being with you."

In his book *Sculpting in Time*, Tarkovsky presents his idea of a poetic cinema as one based upon the reality of the image, upon "pure observation," not symbolism. The film artist "sculpts" in time, reordering and reconstructing the rhythms of life to reveal its deeper meaning. Tarkovksy's book, much of which was written in the last months of his life, is the remarkable testimony of a brave man as well as a great artist. Not surprisingly, given the authoritarian society and censorship he had to overcome, he stresses the importance of freedom and spontaneity, a "fidelity to a personal vision" and uncompromised integrity. Yet Tarkovsky's vision was not limited to individual expression. This is clear when he writes of how our experience of time is transformed by cinematic art: "It becomes tangible when you sense something significant, truthful, going on beyond the events on the screen; when you realize, quite consciously, that what you see in the frame is not limited to its visual depiction, but is a pointer to something stretching out beyond the frame and to infinity." There is, not surprisingly, a humility in this approach: "The image is an impression of the truth, a glimpse of the truth permitted to us in our blindness." We will further explore this transcendent goal of film art in a later chapter.

In the last lines of *Sculpting in Time* Tarkovsky poses provocative questions to the reader: "Perhaps the meaning of all human activity lies in artistic consciousness, in the pointless and selfless creative act? Perhaps our capacity to create is evidence that we ourselves are created in the image and likeness of God?"

The influence and reputation of Tarkovksy, considered by Ingmar Bergman to be "the most important director of our time," has continued to grow. I believe it is Tarkovsky's genuinely idealistic radicalism that has led so many young filmmakers to follow his path; but we must be mindful that, in its search for purity, this path is as dangerous as it is rewarding.

A deeply religious man who was willing to pay a high price for his beliefs, Tarkovsky provides an inspiration for young filmmakers willing to take similar risks.

KRZYSZTOF KIESLOWSKI

As a filmmaker, Krzysztof Kieslowski was both a culmination and an inspiring beginning. He is, in many ways, the fulfillment of the humanist tradition, truthful and compassionate, yet anticipates the ongoing spiritual search evident at the end of the twentieth century. Kieslowski's *Blue, Red,* and *The Double Life of Veronique* confirm the exciting potential of films as an encounter with metaphysical Mystery, and the spiritual principles suggested in this book are manifested in all of his work.

Born in Poland in 1941, Kieslowski's initial work was in documentaries and television. In 1979 he received his first international recognition with his film *Amator,* which won the first prize, ironically, at the Moscow Film Festival. During the 1980s Kieslowski began his long and unique collaboration with Krzysztof Piesiewicz and with composer Zbigniew Preisner. Kieslowski's acknowledgement of Piesiewicz's contributions, for which he was always given screen credit, hints at yet another dimension of collaboration beyond craft concerns; for Piesiewicz, a deeply religious man, was not a writer, but a kind of spiritual companion.

In 1987 they began work on the celebrated ten-part series for Polish television, *The Decalogue,* modern parables on the biblical commandments. This incomparable series has now been shown in film festivals

Irene Jacob in Kieslowski's *Red* (1994)

around the world and is sold as a DVD set in many art museums. Their
remarkable work continued in 1991 with *The Double Life of Veronique*
and culminated in 1993-94 with the *Trois Couleurs* trilogy, *Blue, White,*
and *Red.*

Kieslowski's films are distinguished by a deep sympathy with the human condition that eschews sentimentality, a sense of mystery captured
in the surface of things, and a recognition of the limitations of human
judgment that does not surrender to cynicism. His stated goal was nothing less than "to realize that there is such a thing as a soul."

In *Red,* the final story of the *Tricouleur* trilogy, Kieslowski delves into
one of his most persistent themes: the mysterious ways in which people
are connected. A retired judge, troubled by his years spent judging and
condemning others eavesdrops electronically on his neighbors. He observes their sorrows and follies, now without judgment, or even purpose.
An inexplicable relationship with a young model (she has accidentally

struck his dog with her auto) somehow provokes the judge into confronting his past and leads them both on paths of self-disclosure and forgiveness. (An interesting historical footnote: the judge in *Red* is played by Jean-Louis Trintignant, the actor who, a generation earlier, was the lead in Rohmer's *My Night at Maud's*.)

The strange story of *Red* seems, at times, improbable and ends inconclusively; but Kieslowski's films offer, as he put it, "fragments of life . . . a glimpse of a bit of life without knowing how it began or how it ends." As with Jesus' parables, his stories are subversive and even paradoxical. His strategy was to lead us, as well as his characters to moments of inescapable self-recognition.

In many of his films, such as *Red* and the equally masterful *Blue*, Kieslowski explores the nature of loneliness in the modern world — a paradox, as he sees it, in that we desperately seek privacy, while fearing abandonment. This loneliness marks several of the characters in *The Decalogue* who, living in the same immense and drab public housing complex, nevertheless connect and even help one another.

Kieslowski expanded two of the *Decalogue* episodes into feature length works. *A Short Film About Killing* (1987) addresses the fifth commandment (thou shalt not kill) and again reveals the mysterious relationship between seeming strangers. In this case, a tragic connection emerges. Kieslowski's own terse description is of "a story about a young boy who kills a taxi-driver, and then the law kills the boy." The film is more about the mystery of death than the injustices of capital punishment. The young murderer, we discover, still suffers from the gratuitous death of his young sister. There are clearly multi-levels of meaning in this story, and yet we will never know the "real human reasons," Kieslowski states, why either man dies. Mystery, in this case, through death, touches on the greater mystery of our dialogue with God. *A Short Film About Love* (1988) is an expansion of the sixth in the *Decalogue* series, and critically scrutinizes the contemporary view of love and sex. A young man (Tomek), obsessed with an older, promiscuous woman (Magda), spies on her, and finally confesses his love. She disillusions him with her despairing conviction that the only reality is sex, but, following the shattered young man's unsuccessful attempt at suicide, finds herself now increasingly obsessed with him. Kieslowski has succeeded in his stated objective, for here

Juliette Binoche in Krzysztof Kieslowski's *Blue* (1993)

we find that the most lasting truth in film, as in great fiction, is about the mysterious human capacity for transformation.

Kieslowski relates that this film, more than any other that he made, changed considerably in the cutting room. The film found its coherence only when, recognizing the obsessions of the central characters, all other aspects of reality were then removed. There are few better examples of what I have described as the "mirroring" nature of conflict and drama.

The perspective that Kieslowski desired was "always looking at the world through the eyes of the person who is loving, and not through the eyes of the person who is loved" — a dimension of the *I-Thou* relationship brought to the screen.

There are numerous examples in Kieslowski's work of dialogue on the deepest human level. The tragic past of the doctor in the second *Decalogue* episode, the loss of his own wife and children during the war, is never known to the woman whose unborn child he saves; and yet there is a profound, silent communication between the two. Similarly, we witness the power of unspoken feelings that exist between the betrayed and the betrayers in marriage, as in Kieslowski's Christmas episode, or the potentially disastrous revelation of the true Other that occurs in the episode of the young girl who discovers that the man who has raised her is not her natural father.

There are many such extraordinary moments in Kieslowski's work, some, indeed, as with matters of faith and revelation, beyond description.

Let us conclude with another long shot.

In a broad historical sense, one could say that the films of the second half of the twentieth century were, in varying ways, responses to three great catastrophes: the Holocaust, a revelation of the failure of established "civilized" norms, the Gulag, exposing the moral failure of Communism, and Hiroshima, symbolizing the threat of technological mass destruction. Filmmakers are still struggling with the spiritual implications of these highly symbolic, tragic events. As our survey demonstrates, the most important innovators of modern cinema in the last half century — Bresson, Bazin, Bergman, Fellini, Tarkovsky, and Kieslowski — responded to the hard questions of their times with a deeply religious sensibility. I can only strongly recommend that their work be studied and allowed to guide us.

PART THREE
Spiritual Frontiers

As I believe our historical survey demonstrates, it is the spiritual crisis of the times, more than any mere question of form or aesthetics, that shapes and reveals the frontiers of art. As Eliot observes, new forms are shaped to meet our most pressing needs, individual and social. My further premise is that new creative relationships will be necessary to develop those forms. These are the frontiers I wish to explore.

After working with young people for over two decades — as a teacher and advisor to talented filmmakers, but also as a counselor to homeless men and prison inmates — I'm convinced by the evidence of their yearnings that the most vital need of this generation is to be in union with the transcendent, the one God, the source of inspiration and healing. This is an essential need of every time and generation, of course, but because of the loss of the bonding ties of tradition and family, it now seems acute.

This implies more than a return to religious tradition. We are engaged in a search for the primal springs of art and life itself.

What do we mean by our "need for transcendence"? The word implies "rising above," or "that which is beyond," but, again, as with terms such as *attention* or *evil,* it lies beyond precise definition. Linked to the concepts "holy" or "sacred," transcendence designates that which cannot be named or controlled. Paul Schrader in his excellent book *The Transcendent Style in Film* attempted to render the experience of transcendence into various cinematic components. However, as Schrader himself notes, the experience of transcendence is essentially mysterious. It is non-reductive, the whole not reducible to its parts, much less a given form or style. The experience of the transcendent is beyond aesthetics or the catharsis of drama.

It is perhaps foolhardy to even attempt to explicate what is essentially a mystery. We can, however, validate the word *transcendent* as a legitimate referent to an experience found in all the religious traditions. It has been transmitted, at least partially and sometimes exquisitely, in great painting, poetry, and music, and is now, as Schrader observed, an incipient legacy in the art of film.

If we cannot say precisely what transcendence *is,* we can at least point to what it is like. What are the characteristics of this powerful, time-honored experience?

There are decisive personal experiences, which, while subjective, are universally recognizable. Sometimes called "disclosure situations," they are intense moments of joy, or pain, or fear in which "time stops." This kind of disclosure relates to what theologian David Tracy calls a "limit-experience," in which we encounter the utter "otherness of the whole" as an unfathomable mystery. To speak of a disclosure within limits is to approach the vocabulary of art.

Then there are the communal events such as those related in the Bible that Jewish scholar Emil Fackenheim describes as "root experiences," which constitute the core of a tradition. These are shared experiences of an "awesome reality." They reveal a truth that is so compelling that it ultimately shapes an historical consciousness. Often this consciousness is characterized by a sense of "undifferentiated unity," and events such as those related in the prophetic books of the Bible and the Gospels can unite a people, create holy sites and texts, and, notably, inspire art.

Many in the world of art speak of strikingly similar experiences, but in their own terms. Throughout the ages, the various attempts to describe great art, including the aesthetic experience of beauty, also witness to an awesome unity and a kind of truth claim. Here, also, there is a sense of a "wholeness as a gift of the whole." It is an experience to which the poet Rilke referred when he said that an encounter with a great work of art is "a demand that you change your life."

The common denominator in art and religion involves *the perception of a formal unity that points beyond itself.* But there is still another common experience that seems to contradict this unity. In confronting the highest art, we are often left with a lingering sense of what might be called es-trangement. We have delighted in a great gift, yet at the same time there is a feeling of an incompleteness, of something still missing. This suggests that, paradoxically, the highest purpose of art is to achieve a unity that si-multaneously reveals its radical insufficiency. It can now only point beyond itself; it can now only hint at the glory of its origin. When art reaches a height that evokes the depths of reality, it is akin to revelation, and one senses the mystery of Being itself. We then encounter in art, as in religion, a high wall and a distant call.

Art that shares some of this revelatory power of religion — and it is rare — can be described as *diaphoric,* meaning to "show through," and offers an *epiphany,* a "coming to light." These evocations of a "new light" are the characteristics of what I mean by transcendence.

Transcendence and Modern Culture

If we are to meet the crucial needs of our times, the creative task of the contemporary filmmaker will be to develop forms that render the mysterious and healing presence of God. This exploration forces us, as Eliot prescribes, to "approach the frontiers of ordinary consciousness." This means more than being open to new thoughts and artistic concepts. The task is far more difficult. Our work must also overcome the habituated responses of an audience conditioned by mass media, the noise-induced "sleep" we spoke of at the outset.

In seeking to find formal expressions of the experience of God as transcendent, the artist is engaged in a process of changing nothing less than the consciousness of the modern audience. This is a profound spiritual challenge as well as an artistic one, and, obviously, the arts can't accomplish this transformation alone. It must be part of a larger effort to create what Chiara Lubich describes as "a culture of resurrection," which could also be called "a culture of hope."

An agent of this change of consciousness is already at work. We are seeing an awakening to a more global vision, one that converges cultures and traditions. This may, as some caution, put us at risk of accepting a moral relativism, or a spiritually diluted syncretism, but it is, nonetheless, a significant step in overcoming the barriers of exclusivity and provinciality that have obscured the loving presence of God among all peoples.

As filmmakers, we must expand this unifying vision through our work. We can also enrich this work by "becoming one" with people in the other arts — poetry, music, drama — many of whom are on a similar path. We can find forebears in all the arts to guide us — for instance, great modern poets such as Hopkins, Rilke, Eliot, and Paz. We can aspire to do in our films what has been described as their accomplishment with words: create *signs that point toward a greater reality.*

I believe that the search for transcendence points us, as media artists, in certain directions.

Many filmmakers are now attempting to move beyond the limits of conventional narrative and established film vocabulary. In some cases, this is an attempt to broaden the scope of the medium by creating film po-etry rather than, so to speak, the "prose" of conventional narrative. This is not an entirely new ambition, as it was envisioned and even attempted generations ago by figures as diverse as Cocteau, Vigo, Dovzhenko, Murnau, Auden, and Prevert. The American poet Muriel Rukeyser pre-dicted an energizing convergence of poetry and cinema over a half cen-tury ago.

As with so much of the development of the cinematic art, it is a new direction now made more feasible by technological developments that can extend our reach.

The most serious challenge, however, is to our imagination. To create a complex, yet spontaneous audience response, akin to poetics, means finding significant moments of depth and insight more than forging a progressive narrative. As with poetry, there are moments of truth caught in fleeting images that are more lasting than the fully developed, but of-ten artificial, story line delivering its "message."

The rules of film grammar, including concepts of time and space, as well as linear story continuity, must continue to be reconsidered, and many of the filmmakers that we've cited, and others not mentioned, such as Ozu and Ray, have bravely opened the way for us.

The search for the transcendent, or simply a deeper level of meaning, mandates, I contend, changes in the creative process. For instance, to ex-plore the full depth of a story before fixing its limits requires, in my expe-rience, an intense and often challenging collaborative process.

It is likely, moreover, that the full story and the depth of the characters will appear only during the process of completing the film. This not only suggests that media industry practices, such as those which isolate the writer, must be overcome, but that the writer must be prepared to surrender any self-centered claim on the story. Similarly, to fully reveal "the mystery of the human person," the actors should be integrated into the creative process throughout its development. The "story" of a good film shouldn't really belong to anyone, and establishing this as a shared goal can protect us against the flailings of the proprietary ego, and, even more importantly, can force each artist to explore new and sometimes uncomfortable territory.

To create a film poetry would mean compressing our visual images into what critic James Agee called a "poetry of the commonplace," in which the faces of ordinary people in ordinary circumstances are made translucent. This would require a "shared attention" — a being in the present moment together — in conception, performance, cinematography, and editing.

This is what I mean by "deep collaboration." It is not meant to rival or even reform industry practices, as it has a different objective. Our proposed spiritual and ethical principles can, of course, be applied to the industrial workplace, or, for that matter, any aspect of life. Many fine films have been made, and will continue to be made by determined artists willing to brave the studio system, or who seek the more personal approach of the independent *auteur*. But we should recognize that there is an inescapable tension between these principles and an approach to filmmaking rooted in profit and personal careers. The desire and need for success and personal advancement is understandable in any field, but I've observed that the desire for a Hollywood career is too often an attempt to satisfy a now-compulsive need for recognition. The loss of an authentic self in postmodern culture — a self that can only be sustained by genuine community — has created a desperate demand for attention. But it is an attention that is not attentive. It is "look at me," not "see me." For many of us, it seems more gratifying to star in the movie in our head than to be a day player in God's ongoing drama. In urging a path of "deep collaboration," I'm not, in any case, suggesting art by committee. We should recognize the essential role of exceptional talent, as well as the prerequisite need of artistic discipline. A spiritual exploration, however, requires a collaborative process akin to religious discernment. Such a communal effort will be largely new to us as moderns; yet it is as ancient as art itself, a creative fusion of the spiritual and artistic imagination that lies beyond individual talent and personal expression.

To achieve a true unity as artists, to fuse the essential elements of image, language, music, and design, is to dare to seek the sublime goal evoked by poet Octavio Paz: *We seek to create an encoded silence.*

Epilogue

F or me, this book can't end. It can only pause for reconsiderations.
The artistic goals we seek emanate from a spiritual one: a radically open unity. This is a unity that comes out of a vision of existence as a whole, knowing that the whole is not visible and impossible to fully grasp. But in seeking this One-ness, how are we to live our individual lives? How are we to integrate our lives as artists in media? This has been the central concern in my teaching and in this book. From the vantage of present-day Hollywood, with its intense rivalries and insidious insecurities, this might seem impossible. But it is good to remember that others in the arts, such as the members of theater and dance companies, jazz and chamber ensembles, and choral groups past and present, have long placed group achievements over individual status and ambition.

I can only affirm that it has been done, and it will be done again. The required effort depends, I believe, more on need than desire, more on faith than strength. We ultimately turn to the Other, human and divine, out of necessity, and then community again becomes possible.

What is missing now is what is always missing: a deeper understanding of our shared needs. We suffer from a condition that I call "L.A. loneliness," though it isn't unique to Los Angeles, the real geography of the imagined "Hollywood." This particular form of loneliness, "being alone in a crowd," reflects the prevalent disconnected condition of people around the world. How can we meet this need for community as media artists? Clearly not by offering films with still more anger and estrangement. We must learn to see again without the filter of alienation or self-pity. The language and symbols may vary among religions and cultures, but I believe we share an ancient vision that can guide us. It is that of the "suffering servant" of Isaiah, the Christ, who revealed that our universal need for unity can be achieved only through a loving self-sacrifice.

Filmmakers can use their art to open our eyes, as they have in the past. I end, as I began, in faith: I believe that, together, we can learn to see in a new light.

An Appendix:
Some Personal Reflections on Faith

In my workshops over the years, I've sought that common ground where faith and creative energy converge. In doing so, I've discovered that artists can find at least the start of a spiritual path in the integrity of their work, and that people of all faiths, and many still seeking direction, can be brought together by the principles I've outlined.

My personal belief, my Christian faith, is, however, relevant to everything I do and write. While this book is intended to be inclusive in spirit and accessible to all, I recognize that there are some limits to this accessibility. As it is said, the stained glass window is seen most fully from inside the church. I've thus added this personal note to clarify what I see, again out of experience more than theory, as the relationship of faith and creativity. I'm not a theologian; my observations come from an attempt to unify my own life, work, and beliefs. As this is a universal need, I hope these reflections might be of value to those who do not share my faith or assumptions.

The artistic atmosphere in the Hollywood in which I was raised and worked was, at times, intellectually vigorous, but more often merely reflected the cultural *zeitgeist* of postwar Europe and changing American mores. Most of my friends and teachers, people of honesty and integrity, considered themselves "atheists." This is a term you still hear today, but which has largely lost its meaning. In advocating rational objectivity, the early "free thinkers" fought for an intellectual liberty that was often suppressed by religion. However destructive some of the ultimate consequences, we have all benefited from their labors and sacrifices. But the contemporary "atheist" is one who negates in a vacuum. It makes little sense to proclaim such disbelief unless, as in the past, it is integral to an equation of belief. I would define the atheist of today as "one who doesn't believe in dead gods," yet, increasingly unable to posit a coherent counter belief, is dangerously susceptible to irrationality. The Enlightenment notion of rational order is now as unacceptable to the postmodern "nonbeliever" as biblical revelation. Today's atheist has thus become, ironically, a kind of nostalgic conservative wedded to a romanticized past, a condition not unknown to Christians.

The Hollywood I knew was already in a transition from an era of aggressive and confident alternatives to religious belief, such as socialism or psychotherapy, to a postmodern end-time of empty disbelief. The growing cynicism and despair, so evident in the movies of the seventies, marked the incubation period of my faith. I escaped none of the fears and uncertainties of that time. I was thus molded by the courage and integrity of those whose interpretations of this condition I would ultimately reject.

I want to reflect on some of the central ideas in this book in the light of this personal journey.

The experience of art, especially music, but also including the films that most inspired me, was revelatory in a way that I would come to find akin to religious faith. The noted theologian Hans Urs von Balthasar, whom I read decades later, claimed that without "aesthetic knowledge" — that is, this revelatory experience of beauty — reason and goodness will fade as well. The loss of one transcendental component signals a risk to the classical triad, and to the unity of life itself. But what is the nature of this experience? I came to see it as an encounter with truth.

I'm not a philosopher any more than a theologian, though I'm quite aware of the extended guerilla wars in academia against words such as "beauty," "truth," and, of course, "love." However, Pope John Paul's description of beauty as "the splendor of truth" (in his encyclical *Veritatis Splendor*) is not, for me, an argument, but a testimony that corresponds to my own.

What art, including films, revealed to me was a unity deeper than the disunity of the discordant world around me. In time, as I recognized the inherently narcissistic nature of my imaginative life — like many writers and actors I would eventually turn a neurosis into a profession — I realized the essential need for a discipline. At first I found this in the craft of writing, the ability to impose an artificial structure on the flow of events. But, ultimately, I would see through my own devices. An external discipline, something beyond myself, was needed.

The goal of being in the present moment has become so fashionable that it strikes many as simply New Age cant. But given the narcissism now so prevalent in our media-dominated culture, I came to see it as a vital corrective. This spiritual discipline is simply an effort to connect with a reality deeper than one's own limited self-consciousness.

The paradigm for me as a Christian is, as always, Jesus, who "emptied himself" on the Cross to reveal the ultimate truth of God's redemptive love. This is the model for our spiritual discipline, and if we integrate it into our work, it might be called "creative *kenosis*," an imitation of Jesus' self-emptying in the context of artistic creation. This points to another common denominator between the religious believer and the creative artist: as one who simply tries to "see," and then describe honestly, in whatever form, what is seen.

This "seeing" is in itself an aspect of faith; for belief isn't so much an adherence to abstract thought as it is entering into a living and growing relationship (be-lief, *i.e.*, be-in-life or love). "Let those who have eyes, see," is a biblical demand for attention. For me, being in the present moment is an opening to the awe and wonder essential to art and religion.

The experience of my spiritual companions in different faith traditions, as well as that of my teachers in monastic life, suggests that this self-emptying is best brought about through prayer and flourishes in silence.

I've alluded to a goal of "encoded silence," a phrase of Octavio Paz's about art and poetry, but, for me, a spiritual objective. It is too easy and tempting for us as filmmakers to offer simply more "noise," whether in words or images. Great films, like great music, are composed, as Bresson knew, in large part of significant silence. Spiritually, there is in all of our lives a pain threshold in real silence, whether alone or with others. It's a kind of "silence barrier" that we must try to break. As artists, it means we must think less and listen more.

This silence reveals a longing. We long for something undefined and never wholly recognized. I think that what we are seeking is what Jesus offers. It is the ultimate transformation that comes from the abandonment of the self, and not just the false self, but the self "beneath the mask" as well. This seeming loss reveals the eternal self that is, and is not, the self. This is the code of silence. I find that once we are in this silence, there is nothing more to be said.

Whenever I speak of "embracing the mystery of the Other," I sense Christ's presence; yet I know that this is an experience not limited to people of faith. The idea of Christ as both human and divine, a central Christian mystery, may remain opaque to others; but it is a universal insight when embodied in our deepest encounters with other human beings. Without engaging in theological disputes, we can all come to understand that we share in an incomprehensible unity. This is the depth of being which some of us choose to call divine or holy.

The model for Christians in understanding this mystery is that offered by St. Paul, who discovers himself in a way similar, though with greater depth, to a writer inventing a character or an actor interpreting one. St. Paul discovers who he truly is through his participation in the life of Christ. He finds that "I live now, not I, but Christ lives within me." If we seek in our work to "enter into the Other" with respect and wonder — and the life-giving sexual metaphor is appropriate — we will find the Christ dwelling within us.

Another aspect of this mystery of the Other relates directly to the nature of dialogue. I believe that authentic dialogue — a communication between human beings that goes to levels beyond the merely verbal — reveals the true nature of our consciousness. We come to recognize that our consciousness is interpersonal, and that there is, in reality, no isolated self or sealed subjectivity. For Christians, the illusion of isolation is a sign of sin, or, better, sin itself. At the heart of sin is separation from God. A dialogue governed by love and truth, whether in life or in art, leads us back to an even deeper mystery. When St. Paul spoke of the "Christ within me," he wasn't simply employing a metaphor for his devotion, but was revealing an ontological reality. These extraordinary moments of shared consciousness and insight are what the best of films occasionally capture.

In my workshops, including those conducted with Gil Bailie, I've found that the central concepts of René Girard concerning the historic function of the scapegoat remain highly problematic for many. This is not simply because of the inherent difficulties in understanding Girard's admittedly complex analysis. Girard's ideas help us to differentiate between the sacrificial rituals of archaic religion and myth and the revelation that grew out of the Hebrew prophets, which Christians believe was fulfilled by Jesus. This anthropological understanding we may largely accept; but I find that no one is really comfortable with Girard's further conclusions. The idea that the scapegoat process isn't a distortion of the social order, but provides its very glue, isn't comforting to even the most hardheaded realist.

For Christians, it is particularly painful, given the centrality of the Cross to our faith, to find ourselves as complicit as others in perpetuating the scapegoat mechanism. But if we admit to our victimizing ways as part of our sinfulness, indeed, as a basic element of original sin, we can better understand its ubiquity. The same is true for Girard's insights into mimetic rivalry and envy. Sebastian Moore, a psychologist and priest, has characterized sin as "living in the eyes of others." The operative word in the last two of the Ten Commandments is usually rendered as "covet," but it is our never-ending envy and desires that are being addressed.

Girard's important work lays a foundation for a deeper contemporary understanding of Christian belief; however, there has been an unfortunate tendency to misuse this analysis to justify dubious moral equivalencies in the name of diversity. Those seeking to assert long-established moral principles, albeit sometimes rigidly, are thus vilified as intolerant. The most challenging aspect in all this for filmmakers may prove to be learning "how not to scapegoat the scapegoaters."

While a spirit of solidarity with all human beings must animate us, we should recognize that the idea of solidarity itself has roots in religious tradition. Though frequently violated, the principle is found in the Hebrew *Shema*, the Muslim proclamation of the oneness of God, and the Christian Gospels. Even the concept of the unity of form and content in art is, I believe, derived from the deeper, even more mysterious unity of body and soul. The goal of unity is, therefore, not merely a humanistic vision, but one grounded in the monotheistic tradition as expressed in the prayer of Jesus: "Let them be One, as my Father and I are One." This unity is always at risk. The failures and hypocrisies of religion continue to subvert it; but so does the loss of this tradition and the now fashionable flirtation with neo-pagan polytheism with its latent tribal appeal.

The deepest disunity, however, lies within us. It manifests itself in much of the contemporary culture, and in the isolated state that I observed among my film students, the condition that I've called "L.A. loneliness." I see this as more than social alienation and disconnectedness. This existential loneliness, now so common among the urban young everywhere, signifies an essential loss of meaning. Yet I believe that this in itself is an opportunity to gain understanding. This spiritual isolation is a form of death and an opportunity to begin to understand death in a way that the dominant culture no longer provides, and even evades.

This experience of death as isolation and meaninglessness, however painful, can be of great value, for we will never grasp life or death abstractly. Realism means the integration of death into life. Without this persistent effort, reality is endlessly distorted by fear. This is a crucial perspective for the contemporary artist; for we have no further need of diagnosis or argument if and when we know we're dying. Berdyaev gave wise counsel when he advised us to "treat the dead as living and the living as dying."

I believe we should do our creative work with Lear's words to Cordelia in mind: "As if we were God's spies." We must observe life as if we are the angels in Wim Wenders' marvelous film *Wings of Desire*. But this will, of course, break our hearts. Can we allow our hearts to break? Faith is central to anyone's answer to this question. As Christians, we must struggle against using religion and the concept of God as a defense against this heartbreak. It is the refusal to accept the broken heart — the full reality of suffering and death — that fuels the reign of further suffering and death.

My faith, as I can best understand it, came late and from the experience of profound beauty and devastating loss. My convictions came out of my contradictions. The peace and reconciliation I've been granted come from my belief that the world's vicious cycle of violence and condemnation can be broken — but only by following the path of Christ, the path of a self-sacrificing love. This is at the heart of my faith.

A Second Appendix:
Testing the Principles: *Blue in Green*

A fter a lifetime in Hollywood, observing talented, committed people in creative straightjackets, I became convinced that to meet our deepest needs, and to achieve new techniques in filmmaking, we must seek new relationships.

What might be called an "experiment in unity" came out of my workshops in which I enlisted several highly talented young filmmakers. To the surprise of all involved, our "experiment" became a full-length feature, *Blue in Green.*

It has been argued that the term "experimental art" is redundant because all art is experimental by nature, in that each work is a search for a proper, yet largely undetermined form. Nonetheless, *Blue in Green* can be described as genuinely experimental in that it was a conscious exploration of a process that was an end in itself; that is, we did not strive for any specific result. Our objective was simply to challenge ourselves by attempting a highly, even provocatively collaborative process.

The experiment began with what we called a "story vision," simply an idea or inspiration about a possible film. The group's initial story visions all came from intriguing real-life incidents. We realized, however, that the nature of what became the *Blue in Green* story, an all-night party, suggested the further possibility of a highly collaborative approach. The actors would be encouraged to originate their characters, and the dialogue, while based on extensive preparation, was to be wholly improvised. We then allowed the "vision" to develop and deepen through some intense group discussions over several weeks.

The project, from the outset, "belonged" to no one, or, better yet, to everyone.

Here is a summary of the *Blue in Green* premise: A young woman in her thirties, desperately hoping to find a mate, is convinced that the man with whom she has had an intimate but brief relationship is the right one for her. She plans to introduce him to her friends at her birthday party. Everyone is curious and eager to meet this new man — but he never comes.

The substance of the piece lies in its insights into the woman and her friends, and an exploration of the desires and fears of everyone at the party. *Blue in Green* is a study of universal loneliness, but it subtly reveals a spiritual search as well.

The creative process quickly became a testing of the limits of radical collaboration. A small core group of people willing to unite their individual talents worked on the project from beginning to end, a unique merging of directors, writers, cinematographers, editors, actors — and a poet. There was no shooting script; however, the characters were carefully developed in rehearsal. This improvisational approach produced, as we hoped, some remarkable surprises, some significantly altering the story, much of which was then "written" in the editing process.

The actors were integrated into the project through improvisational techniques largely based upon Viola Spolin's "games" — a process that involved both cast and crew. This approach allowed each actor the freedom and confidence to create his or her own character. Similarly, we asked the jazz musicians who composed the score to begin their work by joining us in the rehearsal period. The score was recorded in two sessions, the first before the editing was completed. Some of the film was then cut to music.

Of our three spiritual principles, perhaps the one that proved most crucial was being in the present moment. Clearly, the improvisational approach required intense concentration on the part of the actors, but everyone involved had to maintain attention. This was necessary not only to determine the value of a take, but, also, in that there was no script, to maintain a vision of the developing story. The cinematographers were required to be "in the moment" with the performers if they were to anticipate, sometimes within seconds, what shot or angle would be needed.

The mystery of the Other was inherent, I believe, in the story vision itself. Each character's deepest desires came to the surface, at times in unpredictable ways that would have been stifled by anything less than a freedom to "allow them to be."

The most radical commitment, however, was to work together in a manner that would recognize the equal worth and contribution of all involved. This meant "transforming conflict," and, perhaps not surprisingly, this proved to be the most difficult practice to sustain. The process stumbled and stalled at times as we attempted to take conflicts to deeper levels where they could be more honestly confronted. We suffered some painful setbacks in this effort, but what we learned from the difficulties may prove to be the most valuable lesson of all. In the end, we believe we learned two important things: The process is very difficult and requires a strong spiritual foundation; but, with commitment, it can work, and is a path filled with possibilities.

For more information on *Blue in Green* and on the Unica Collaborative, visit the website at www.blue-in-green.com.

Filmography

This filmography includes over a hundred twentieth-century films, a sampling that I believe serves to illustrate how the development of the cinematic art reflected the spiritual and moral concerns of the time. It features a wide range of films drawn from twenty countries and includes some silent classics and several comedies, though few Hollywood genre films and no musicals. As with the historical survey, it is highly selective and admittedly omits many fine films.

I have tried to view these films through the lens of the principles suggested in this book. While the perspective of several works could be called despairing, I don't believe that any succumb to cynicism or the fashionable nihilism so evident in the last decades of the century. Many are highly critical of their societies, yet none, in my opinion, evade the central concerns through scapegoating. Not all of these films offer a clear response to the crises they reflect, morally or otherwise, but each in its own way deepened our understanding, and did so with considerable artistry.

For the convenience of the reader, I have alphabetized the list, and, whenever relevant, I have also cited the screenwriters and source material following the name of the director.

American Graffiti (USA, 1973) George Lucas

A Nous la Liberté (France, 1931) René Clair

Andrei Rublev (Russia, 1966) Andrei Tarkovsky

The Apartment (USA, 1960) Billy Wilder/I. A. L. Diamond

The Apu Trilogy (India, 1955-59) Satyajit Ray

Ashes and Diamonds (Poland, 1958) Andrzej Wajda

Au Revoir les Enfants (France, 1987) Louis Malle

Babette's Feast (Denmark, 1987) Gabriel Axel/I. Dinesen

The Best Years of Our Lives (USA, 1946) William Wyler/R. Sherwood &
  M. Kantor

Bicycle Thieves (Italy, 1947) V. De Sica/C. Zavattini

Black Robe (USA, 1991) Bruce Beresford/Brian Moore

Blue (Poland/France, 1993) K. Kieslowski

Breaking the Waves (Denmark, 1996) L. von Trier/P. Asmussen

Brief Encounter (UK, 1946) David Lean/Noel Coward

Broken Blossoms (USA, 1919) D. W. Griffith

The Burmese Harp (Japan, 1956) Kon Ichikawa

Celebration (Sweden, 1998) T. Vinterberg/H. Rukov

Chariots of Fire (UK, 1981) Hugh Hudson/Colin Welland

Children of Paradise (France, 1945) Marcel Carné/Jacques Prevert

Chinatown (USA, 1974) Roman Polanski/Robert Towne

Chloe in the Afternoon (France, 1972) Eric Rohmer

Citizen Kane (USA, 1941) Orson Welles/Herman Mankiewicz

City Lights (USA, 1931) Charles Chaplin

Crimes and Misdemeanors (USA, 1988) Woody Allen

Day of Wrath (Sweden, 1943) Carl Dreyer

The Decalogue (Poland, 1987) K. Kieslowski

Diary of a Country Priest (France, 1950) R. Bresson/G. Bernanos

Distant Voices, Still Lives (UK, 1988) Terence Davies

La Dolce Vita (Italy, 1960) Federico Fellini

The Double Life of Veronique (Poland/France, 1991) K. Kieslowski

Earth (Russia, 1930) Aleksandr Dovzhenko

The Easy Life (Italy, 1962) Dino Risi

Elephant Man (UK, 1980) David Lynch/C. De Vore, E. Bergren

Eroica (Poland, 1958) Andrzej Munk/J. Stawinski

Fanny and Alexander (Sweden, 1983) Ingmar Bergman

Four Hundred Blows (France, 1958) François Truffaut

The Garden of the Finzi-Continis (Italy, 1970) V. De Sica/G. Bassani

The General (USA, 1927) Clyde Bruckman & Buster Keaton

The Godfather, Parts I & II (USA, 1972-74) F. F. Coppola/Mario Puzo

The Gold Rush (USA, 1925) Charles Chaplin

The Gospel According to Matthew (Italy, 1964) Pier Paolo Pasolini

Grand Illusion (France, 1937) Jean Renoir/Charles Spaak

The Grapes of Wrath (USA, 1940) John Ford/N. Johnson/J. Steinbeck

Greed (USA, 1924) Erich von Stroheim/Frank Norris

Gregory's Girl (Scotland, 1981) Bill Forsyth

La Guerre est Finie (France, 1966) Alain Resnais/Jorge Semprún

Ikiru (Japan, 1952) Akira Kurosawa/Shinobu Hashimoto

In Cold Blood (USA, 1967) Richard Brooks/Truman Capote

Jesus of Montreal (Canada, 1989) Denys Arcand

Jules et Jim (France, 1961) François Truffaut/J. Gruault/H.-P. Roché

Loves of a Blonde (Czechoslovakia, 1965) Milos Forman

Magnolia (USA, 1998) Paul Thomas Anderson

A Man Condemned to Death Escapes (France, 1956) R. Bresson

A Man for All Seasons (UK, 1966) Fred Zinnemann/Robert Bolt

Marty (USA, 1955) Delbert Mann/Paddy Chayefsky

Melvin and Howard (USA, 1980) Jonathan Demme/Bo Goldman

Mephisto (Hungary, 1981) Istvan Szábó/Klaus Mann

Midnight Cowboy (USA, 1969) J. Schlesinger/W. Salt/J. L. Herlihy

The Miracle (Italy, 1948) Roberto Rossellini/Federico Fellini

Miracle in Milan (Italy, 1951) V. De Sica/C. Zavattini

The Mirror (Russia, 1975) Andrei Tarkovsky

Modern Times (USA, 1937) Charles Chaplin

My Left Foot (Ireland, 1980) J. Sheridan/S. Connaughton/C. Brown

My Man Godfrey (USA, 1936) Gregory La Cava/M. Ryskind & E. Hatch

Network (USA, 1976) Sidney Lumet/Paddy Chayefsky

My Night at Maud's (France, 1969) Eric Rohmer

Ninotchka (USA, 1939) Ernst Lubitsch/B. Wilder, W. Reisch, C. Brackett

Los Olvidados (Mexico, 1950) Luis Buñuel

On the Waterfront (USA, 1954) Elia Kazan/Budd Shulberg

One Flew Over the Cuckoo's Nest (USA, 1975) M. Forman/B. Goldman/
    K. Kesey

8½ (*Otto e Mezzo*, Italy, 1962) Federico Fellini

Pandora's Box (Germany, 1929) G. W. Pabst/F. Wedekind

The Passion of Joan of Arc (Denmark, 1926) Carl Dreyer

Pickpocket (France, 1959) Robert Bresson

Pixote (Brazil, 1981) Hector Babenco

Places in the Heart (USA, 1984) Robert Benton

Playtime (France, 1973) Jacques Tati

Il Posto (Italy, 1961) Ermanno Olmi

The Quarrel (Canada, 1990) E. Cohen/D. Brandes/J. Telushkin

Rashomon (Japan, 1951) Akira Kurosawa

Red (Poland/France, 1994) K. Kieslowski

Rules of the Game (France, 1939) Jean Renoir/Carl Koch

Seventh Seal (Sweden, 1957) Ingmar Bergman

Schindler's List (USA, 1993) Steven Spielberg/S. Zalian

Shadows (USA, 1959) John Cassavetes

La Strada (Italy, 1954) Federico Fellini

Sullivan's Travels (USA, 1941) Preston Sturges

Sunrise (Germany/USA, 1927) F. W. Murnau/Hermann Sudermann

Taxi Driver (USA, 1976) Martin Scorsese/Paul Schrader

Tender Mercies (USA, 1983) Bruce Beresford/Horton Foote

Thérèse (France, 1986) Alain Cavalier/Camille de Casabianca

The Third Man (UK, 1949) Carol Reed/Graham Greene

Tokyo Story (Japan, 1953) Yasujiro Ozu/Kôgo Noda

Treasure of the Sierra Madre (USA, 1948) John Huston/B. Traven

The Tree of the Wooden Clogs (Italy, 1978) Ermanno Olmi

True Confessions (USA, 1981) Ulu Grosbard/John Gregory Dunne

2001: A Space Odyssey (USA, 1968) Stanley Kubrick/Arthur Clarke

Umberto D (Italy, 1952) V. De Sica/C. Zavattini

El Verdugo (Spain, 1963) Luis Berlanga/R. Azcona & E. Flaiano

Il Vitelloni (Italy, 1953) Federico Fellini

Virgin Spring (Sweden, 1957) Ingmar Bergman

Wild Strawberries (Sweden, 1957) Ingmar Bergman

Wings of Desire (Germany, 1987) Wim Wenders/Peter Handke

The Year of Living Dangerously (Australia, 1982) P. Weir/C. J. Koch

Zéro de Conduite (France, 1933) Jean Vigo

As evidence of their considerable influence, there have been several documentaries now made about Tarkovsky and Kieslowski. Michal Leszczylowski's *Directed by Andrei Tarkovsky* shows Tarkovsky at work on *The Sacrifice* and Chris Marker documented his last days and reflections in *A Day
in the Life of Andrey*. A film tribute to Kieslowski was produced by his
friend Agnieszka Holland following his death and a later profile was made
in 2006 by Doug Cummings.

Acknowledgments

I have placed these acknowledgments at the end of this book for two reasons. I thought that a citation of my many sources would possibly be more helpful after reading the contents, and it would allow me further space to express the gratitude I owe to so many.

The initial inspiration for this book came from my spiritual brother, Paul Wolff, an ordained storyteller in the Jewish tradition, who envisioned a new path for filmmaking and encouraged me to follow it. Our brothers in interfaith dialogue — psychologist Jim Carolla and Rabbi Scott Shapiro — contributed significantly to the formation of the spiritual foundations of the book, particularly the principle of Being in the Present Moment. This principle was also fundamental to the work of my acting teacher, Viola Spolin, a visionary whose book *Improvisational Theater* remains invaluable.

The second principle, concerning the mystery of the Other, has been articulated most fully by Martin Buber in his classic *I and Thou*. The core of this principle was then illuminated for me by Chiara Lubich's compassionate understanding of "Jesus Forsaken," expressed in her book *The Cry.* Her prophetic insight reveals that the true mystery of the Other is ultimately grasped only by entering into the depth of our shared suffering.

My frequent citations of Simone Weil indicate my indebtedness to that most original thinker. My understanding of her concept of tragedy is derived from Katherine T. Brueck's fine book *The Redemption of Tragedy: The Literary Tradition of Simone Weil.* The insights of Franz Rosenzweig came from another excellent book, *Idolatry and Representation* by Leora Batnitzky.

The work of René Girard and the exploration of his theories by my good friend Gil Bailie was not only essential to the development of the third principle, transforming conflict, but provided a moral and intellectual stimulation for the whole book. I cannot separate Gil's writing from my own in that chapter, and hope that he will accept this admission as a form of thanks. I recommend *The Girard Reader* as an introduction to that notable scholar's work, as well as Gil's book *Violence Unveiled*.

A version of the "Spiritual Frontiers" chapter appeared originally in *Image* Quarterly, and Gregory Wolfe, the editor, has been kind and brave enough to print several of my articles over the years. I owe him thanks for this encouragement, as well as sincere appreciation for his dedication to his own faith-filled work. His colleague at *Image*, Mary Kenagy, has my gratitude for her skillful editing.

I want to thank my many *amici* in the Focolare Movement, particularly Mary Cass and Michele Zanzucchi, as well as Barbara Nicolosi of Act One, Scott Young of the City of Angels Festival, and Michael Feeley, Leah Buturain-Schneider, Sister Margaret Devlin, Father Alexei Smith, and my other Windhover Forum companions for providing numerous occasions for me to articulate the ideas in this book, and for their patience as I did so. John Furia offered me the opportunity to teach at the USC (University of Southern California) film school for several years, an opportunity almost as valuable as his invaluable friendship.

My fellow writers in Hollywood taught me as much about life and commitment as they did about movies. My longtime partner, Jim Buchanan, remains my valued mentor, proving by example that an honest man can survive and be widely respected in Hollywood. Frank Thompson and our several companions at his writers' roundtable, a movable feast for over twenty years, have offered me lasting gifts of their intelligence and wit. My thanks to all of these fellow survivors.

If my work achieves any integrity, it will be largely due to another old friend, George Moore, a scientist with an artist's sensibility who has tried to keep me intellectually honest over a shared lifetime. If I faltered, it was not for George's lack of effort.

Blue in Green wasn't conceived as the final culmination of an experiment, but as its beginning, and the spiritual steps suggested in this book are merely starting points. Where they will lead will depend upon the next generation.

I have been blessed with many exceptional students who became, in time, friends. Among them were those in the "Unica Collaborative" who created *Blue in Green*. For their dedication, I thank each of them: Malia Fields, Zak Forsman, Laura Laurent, David Melvin, and Kevin Shah. My "old pro" friends, Jerry Cotts and Phil Fehrle, gave us generous help and advice, and Priya Kumar, Joel and Rebecca Russell, and David Tlapek contributed to the early development. I offer my sincere thanks to all of them, to the excellent cast, and the marvelous Tierney Sutton Band. And a special thanks to Laura Laurent for her thoughtful personal assistance.

I want to also express my appreciation to Sandra de Groot and all of the Eerdmans publishing family for their considerate support and guidance. I'm also indebted to Howard and Tookie Schuyler for their patient help in arranging the photos.

My final thanks is the most impossible to express, and so I wish to simply acknowledge that I could not have written this book without the friendship and help of Gabriel Meyer.

My late wife Ruth would have been pleased that I have finally written a book. She and my daughters, Teresa and Bethe, are part of everything I do in life, and always will be.

And the darkness could not extinguish the Light.

The Gospel of John, Chapter One